Savvy
Dealing with people, power and politics at work

For John

Savvy
Dealing with people, power and politics at work

JANE CLARKE

KoganPage

LONDON PHILADELPHIA NEW DELHI

First published in Great Britain and the United States in 2012 by Kogan Page Limited

120 Pentonville Road
London N1 9JN
United Kingdom
www.koganpage.com

1518 Walnut Street, Suite 1100
Philadelphia PA 19102
USA

4737/23 Ansari Road
Daryaganj
New Delhi 110002
India

© Jane Clarke, 2012

ISBN   978 0 7494 6526 1
E-ISBN 978 0 7494 6527 8

British Library Cataloguing-in-Publication Data

A CIP record for this book is available from the British Library.

Library of Congress Cataloging-in-Publication Data

Clarke, Jane.
  Savvy : dealing with people, power and politics at work / Jane Clarke.
    p. cm.
  ISBN 978-0-7494-6526-1 – ISBN 978-0-7494-6527-8   1. Office politics.
2. Conflict management.   3. Interpersonal relations.   I. Title.
  HF5386.5.C574 2012
  650.1'3–dc23
                                                        2012001492

Typeset by Graphicraft Ltd, Hong Kong
Print production managed by Jellyfish
Printed and bound by CPI Group (UK) Ltd, Croydon, CR0 4YY

Contents

Foreword

For me, the moment anyone uses the word 'politics' in business I want to run for the hills. But actually this isn't about politics at all – that's just an office terminology – this is about being savvy. About having positive relationships in the workplace and using them to get the outcome required for the advancement of your career, personal happiness and the success of the business.

I left corporate life to set up my own business, because I couldn't deal with office 'politics.' Little did I know then it was because I simply did not know how to. If only I'd had this book!

In my latter years as Creative Director at Harvey Nichols, most of my time was spent lobbying. I was the ideas generator and the change person; that was my job – but the Board was all about consensus. I thought that if I had the vision, and really flew the flag, other people should feel the same way. But that didn't happen. I got into the position where I wasn't developing ideas, just lobbying. Instead of fighting the system, I should have played it.

Fifteen years into my own business, and with several TV series and a Government project under my belt, I can safely say the need for negotiation never goes away. The pace of politics is painfully slow. I feel my chest contracting as I think about it.

I now have 50 people working for me and I'm doing it with them. And they must be doing it with me.

These days, when people tell me, "That's a mad idea," WHAT IS A MAD IDEA is I feel confident enough about who I am to just go with it. I couldn't do that in the past. Or could I? What would I have done differently if this book was around then?

This book is like business therapy – like a really great session with a therapist who cares about you. It helps you to understand that dealing with the politics is just about work behaviours which get the most out of yourself and out of other people – your bosses and the team.

It's learning about how to get through your working life and, most importantly, make it enjoyable. It's about knowing your strengths and surrounding yourself with people who complement your strengths (and compensate for your weaknesses). And in a leadership position, it's all about the skills to get harmony and focus and balance others' energies. This is all so vital; I wish I'd learnt it all earlier. You wouldn't walk down the street naked, so don't walk into the office naked! Read this book.

Mary Portas

Acknowledgements

I would like to acknowledge the contribution of my colleagues at Nicholson McBride, who have been highly supportive throughout the process of writing this book – from concept stage to final proofs. Most notably, thanks are due to Kate Brown, Rubina Patel, Emma Seward, Francesca King, Ruth Colling, Helen Fisher, Emily Fröhlich, Nick Kambitsis, Kath Timmins and Geraldine Whitehouse. John Nicholson, as ever, has been instrumental in inputting ideas, editing and proofing. So too has Edward Creasy, whose support and criticism have been invaluable. Dan Westlake at Artsgraphica partnered with us in developing the office politics survey. Thanks are also due to Susannah Lear, without whom there would be no book, to Sharon Walker for her tireless efforts on my behalf and to Mary Portas for her words of wisdom. I also owe a significant debt to the team at Kogan Page. Finally, I am immensely grateful to the many friends and clients who have contributed to the research, whose names I have not listed here due to the sometimes controversial nature of the stories they told, and to the many thousands who took part in the online survey. Your views and case studies have made this book.

Introduction

Hard times breed bad behaviour. An informal survey, conducted at the height of the global financial crisis, indicated that almost 100 per cent of the respondents had noticed an increase in the level of politicking in their place of work. You may say that this is inevitable: it is well known that office politics increases in times of change, particularly when people are fearful – and rising unemployment, austerity measures and global financial uncertainty hardly make for a stable, positive work environment!

Changes in the way in which we work are also inflaming the situation. Technology enables us to communicate, instantaneously, with large numbers of people all over the world: one result of this is an exponential increase in the scope for error. How many of us have found ourselves in a scrape after forwarding an e-mail by mistake, or 'replying to all' without first checking who all the original recipients are? More sinister is what people who have negative motives can now do with technology. Cyber-bullying has become rife: people's lives and careers can be destroyed by information posted on the internet – with very little accountability on the part of the perpetrator.

Our recent research findings are peppered through the book, but one is worth flagging right at the outset: at the time of writing, more than 37 per cent of people say they have witnessed bullying at work in the last 12 months. As consultants, my colleagues and I can bear witness to a significant increase in reports of bullying, deceit and manipulation in the last few years.

As a result of all these changes, it seems fair to conclude that political savvy is a commodity whose value is increasing. Research carried out by executive search firms has long identified political savvy as a critical skill for those who want to progress up the career ladder. The problem is that many people don't possess it – and some say they don't *want* to possess it. So the challenge is to establish a way of succeeding in business without compromising values or integrity. For me, this is made all the more difficult by the fact that I have never been very good at playing the politics. In fact, I'd probably go so far as to say that I have no natural aptitude! I was always in trouble at my previous company – a large financial services conglomerate – for talking or acting out of turn, and was frequently asked to account for my behaviour. When I decided to leave in order to join a consultancy practice, my boss at the time, as a parting gift, offered my new boss the advice that he would need to teach me some tact. Uncomfortable though this made me, it also provided an incentive to start dissecting the art of office politics, by establishing who were the effective office politicians and what constituted political savvy.

In this book I have tried to construct a positive, but realistic, approach to the subject, in order to provide a handbook for people who want a better understanding of office politics and how to make things happen. It's for readers who want to hone their political savvy without compromising their values or integrity. Of course, there's always a danger of political savvy being abused – either deliberately or unknowingly. But I would hope that, when this happens, people who have read this book will be in a position to counter, deal with, or at the very least be aware of, what's going on – in a business world searching for a new code of conduct to replace the values which failed to prevent the banking crisis of 2008, and still undermine efforts to create a less hazardous working environment.

Chapter One
What is savvy?

Political savvy – definition

Understands and utilizes the dynamics of power, organization, and decision making to achieve objectives

US Department of Health & Human Services

Look up the word 'savvy' in a dictionary and you will find words like 'nous', 'savoir-faire', 'sense' and 'ability'. But the ability to do what? People who display savvy have an uncanny knack of anticipating problems and complications. They seem to know what's around the corner. And when challenges materialize, they read the politics of the situation quickly and accurately, and know exactly what to do: they talk to their contacts and take the necessary actions, reassuring stakeholders and solving problems as they go.

For the purposes of this book, we define savvy as the ability to deal effectively with politics at work. So we need first to explore what office politics actually is. One thing's for sure: office politics usually gets bad press. For example, most people who took part in our survey say that a political animal is someone who:

- claims the credit for successes – whether or not they actually contributed;
- makes quite sure that they never, ever get the blame when things go wrong;

- has no qualms about stitching up the competition, whether the 'enemy' works for another company or is a colleague who sits in the next office;
- is excellent at managing up the line, but not so bothered about the people who work for them;
- would never allow the objective truth to get in the way of a career-enhancing manoeuvre.

Interestingly, when people are asked, their overwhelming view is that playing the politics is something *other people* do! All round, it appears to be a negative thing. But is it? It certainly wasn't always that way. The word 'politics' is derived from the ancient Greek word *polis*, which means city state – the organizational structure introduced to help create some order in a society with many diverse, and sometimes conflicting, interests. But doesn't that describe all societies? And come to think of it, couldn't that also be said of most organizations?

So a question presents itself: are all organizations political? Think about your company and answer the following questions:

- Is money tight?
- Are there more jobs at the bottom of the corporate ladder than there are at the top?
- Do some people appear to have more 'clout' than their position in the food chain merits – and more than others of identical grade?
- Are some individuals always better informed about what's going on than others?
- Do people have different interests – both corporate and personal?
- Does decision making tend to take place through informal channels?

If the answer to any of these questions – let alone all of them – is yes, then your organization *is* political. And it's a rare company that fails to score at least five out of six. Indeed, there's a school of thought that believes that if more than two people are involved in *anything*, there is a political dimension and therefore a political dynamic which must be managed.

How do people perceive the politics?

So office politics is a fact of life. But is it *always* negative? Certainly, most dictionary definitions carry pejorative and sinister connotations. Office politics is something devious and under-hand. It's about advancing your own agenda at the expense of others and of the organization's goals. But views are changing: I can make this assertion with confidence because we have it in two surveys, carried out 13 years apart. In 1998, 80 per cent of people described office politics as being destructive rather than constructive. In 2011, this had reduced to around half, which is just as well when you consider that over 60 per cent believe political savvy has become more important as a skill generally – a figure which increases to a massive 74 per cent when you're talking about career progression (with men more likely to hold this view than women). If you add into the equation the 60 per cent who observe that politicking is on the increase, you can see that savvy becomes vitally important.

And in terms of how office politics is defined, views on that have changed too. In our previous study, respondents generally used words and phrases like *manipulating, manoeuvring, string pulling, game playing, back-stabbing, bitching, buck passing, bullying, sucking up, putting down, claiming success* and *diverting blame*. Today, people have broadened their perception of what office politics is all about: 71 per cent agreed with the definition that it is merely the informal, rather than the formal, way of getting things done. Certainly, the assumption that office politics is covert rather than overt is well accepted. As one person described it:

> The definition is getting broader as organizations become more sophisticated. It started as a negative – people playing games for their own purpose and, if they were cute about it, others didn't know about it until it was too late. It's now become almost a part of how business is done. It's assumed that there is a game to play and sometimes that can be a positive, provided you know that's the sort of arena you're in, and you are aware of who to engage with, who to get on side and where the stumbling blocks are going to be.

Interestingly, whilst 71 per cent of people agreed with the definition of the informal, rather than the formal, way of getting things done, the nearest percentages after that were:

- saying one thing and doing another: 47 per cent;
- talking behind people's backs: 46 per cent;
- doing things for others that you don't have to for personal gain: 38 per cent.

Clearly, the negative connotations haven't disappeared altogether. Only 27 per cent thought that 'working collaboratively' was anything to do with office politics!

So it's the stuff that the induction programme doesn't tell you – activities that are outside your job description, that you just have to pick up by being alert, watching the experts and learning how to read the runes. But more than that, office politics implies the acquisition and utilization of power to achieve your personal ambitions. This practice can be either constructive or destructive. It can be driven by selfless concern for the general corporate good or by purely selfish motives: on the one hand, public spirited; on the other, entirely self-seeking. So you need to interpret whether an individual is working the system to get a result for the organization or merely for themselves.

Take a look at Table 1.1.

TABLE 1.1

Negative view of the politics	Generous view of the politics
She is incredibly manipulative.	She is very influential.
They're such a political team.	We're just trying to get the job done.
'Divide and rule' is the game around here.	A degree of internal competition is motivating.
The grapevine is rife.	I try to keep myself informed about what's going on – and I tip others off when I think it's necessary.
The people who get promotion around here are the boss's favourites.	The people who get promotion are those who help the boss to achieve his/her objectives – and those of the team.
It's not what you know, but who you know.	It's important to network with people across the business.
They're up to something.	I can't wait to hear the new direction of the company.

The left-hand side contains comments you would expect to hear from people who have a negative view of politics. An alternative view of the same situation is represented on the other side. People will interpret things differently according to their position and their state of mind.

Why do views differ?

The reasons why you might fall into one camp or the other can be diverse:

- Are you the victim or are you the perpetrator?
- Are you on the inside or the outside?
- Do you consider politics to be a fact of life or an unnecessary evil?
- Are you good at the politics or is it not your great strength?
- Is your company a great place to work or a nightmare?
- Is there a lot of politics around or not too much?

Each of these questions is explored in more depth below.

'I'm a victim' vs 'I'm the perpetrator'

First, are you the perceived perpetrator or are you the victim of the politics? If it's you, or your team, who are the instigators, you are far more likely to be generous in your account of events, while observers, or those on the receiving end, will tend to be more negative. It's important to recognize, however, that you might cause trouble unwittingly. In other words, you could be the perpetrator, without meaning any harm – or even realizing it! For instance, you decide that you can't really be bothered to inform a whole load of people about what you've been up to, because you don't have time, or because they don't really 'need to know', and then something goes wrong because of your omission. You are hardly behaving like Machiavelli, but you may well have stirred up the proverbial hornets' nest. By contrast, you might be fully aware of the injury you are about to cause, but feel that your behaviour is justified, because the other person has it coming to them, or because it is either you or them, or because you are feeling mischievous – or any one of a myriad of other reasons. Suffice it to say that the way you feel about any situation will depend on whether you are the victim or the perpetrator – and your motives for acting the way you did.

'I'm on the inside' vs 'I'm on the outside'

The feeling of being in the A-team or the B-team, an insider or an outsider, at the core or on the periphery, is common in organizational life. Most bosses, at some point or other in their careers, have been accused of demonstrating favouritism. And if you don't consider yourself to be the blue-eyed boy or girl, you may well complain that there are politics at work, and feel at a disadvantage or even victimized. You may observe peers who, in your view, contribute less than you do and perform worse but who are consistently praised more highly for what they do. It is of course acceptable – even desirable – for a manager to focus on certain individuals, eg new team members or those facing a particular challenge, provided that this attention is switched regularly to allow everyone to have their 'time in the sun'.

These considerations apply more broadly when it comes to the politics of the whole organization. Where are the decisions being taken? Where do you need to work in order to have a meaningful input? Where does the power really lie? Quite often, those who work outside head office feel disadvantaged by the balance of power. They constantly battle with edicts from on high, feel that no one consulted them, and as a consequence they just don't see the sense of what they've been asked to do. They struggle to understand the methods, and fail to buy into the values. The power lies at the centre – well, that's the perception – and people might yearn to belong to it, or rebel against it.

'Politics is a fact of life' vs 'Politics is an unnecessary evil'

The third factor relates to your perception of politics. Over the years, I have run many hundreds of workshops for people who say they would like to become more savvy. The vast majority of these people volunteer to attend the programme, so you might argue that the desire for change is there. But is it? Once in the room, most people say that they have an inbuilt abhorrence of office politics and, by choice, they wouldn't engage in politicking at all. Many of these people have been given what has been positioned as negative feedback in their appraisals, largely revolving around keeping their heads down, expecting their results to speak for themselves, not building their profile and failing to network. The individuals acknowledge that the feedback is accurate but, at some level, don't want to change, because compliance would – in their view – constitute sacrificing their values: it's just not how they see themselves.

It sounds obvious, but successive studies clearly indicate that those people who consider it important to understand and work the politics are also those who hold the most positive and constructive view of what it can do for an organization. Those who can't be bothered with politics, or can't even bear the thought of it, consider politicking to be destructive and unhelpful. This personal view will undoubtedly have a bearing on whether the individual falls into the left- or the right-hand column of Table 1.1. Interestingly, our recent survey has shown that, whilst 70 per cent of men consider themselves to be politically savvy, the percentage is massively lower for women: only 50 per cent. Potential reasons for this gender split are also revealed by the survey results. More on that later.

'This is something I'm good at' vs 'This is not my great strength'

Clearly, mindset and attitude have a bearing on how much you're prepared to engage with the politics, but they also impact on how accomplished you are at playing the politics – your savvy. It comes very naturally to some people to exert persuasion, build networks and make things happen. They actually enjoy the interpersonal side of their work and get a kick out of observing and influencing others' behaviour. For others, this is just an ordeal; they don't enjoy it and they're not good at it.

'This is a great place to work' vs 'This place is a nightmare'

Another factor is the climate of the organization. Companies with a great deal of negative political activity tend to be characterized by poor morale, low trust and a lack of openness. In these circumstances, people are likely to be distrustful of motives, there will be a feeling of 'us and them' and rumours will be rife. But don't be misled: office politics still goes on in companies with open and trusting climates, in which people are highly motivated. It's just that the associated behaviours tend to be described more positively – as actively influencing decisions, communicating effectively and networking, for instance.

'There's not too much of it around' vs 'There's a lot of it around'

The final factor is related to the scale of the problem – just how much destructive politicking goes on around here? We've established that office politics, in its broadest sense, is at work in all organizations. But it would be inaccurate to suggest that political activity is always on the same scale. Some are far more prone to negative politicking.

Why are some companies more political?

Companies at the high end of the scale (and probably the ones with problems in this area) are likely to be those where some or all of the following apply:

- excessive competition at the top;
- ambiguous goals;
- complex structures;
- no clear definition of performance;
- high level of change;
- refusal by powerful people to change;
- punishment culture;
- limited resources;
- jobs at risk.

Glance down the list and it will become apparent that these factors are far more likely to prevail in times of turbulence and difficulty: one reason why we are seeing higher levels of politicking in organizations today. So let's examine these further.

Excessive competition at the top: 'Why can't they get on?'

Although it often comes as a surprise to people in very senior positions, tensions, rifts and competition at executive level are usually patently clear to everyone. People talk openly about the fact that X and Y can't stand one another and it often becomes a standing joke. This obviously causes a number of problems. People are asked to nail their flag to one mast or another, demonstrating where their loyalties really lie, which inevitably creates competition lower down the organization. Furthermore, these tensions inevitably lead to confusion about the overall strategy and direction of the company. Conflicts of interest and personality are likely to become common – not to mention a weakening of the leadership's credibility. This type of executive conflict can, however, sometimes have a 'positive' knock-on effect – the people below them unite against what they consider to be the 'common enemy': the leadership team. Not much consolation, of course, so it's probably better to ensure that the senior people are aligned.

Ambiguous goals: 'What are we aiming for here?'

It is critically important to ensure that everyone understands clearly what they are supposed to be achieving. Whilst this sounds obvious, it is surprising how many organizations lack this clarity – and people just get on with doing what they think is best. When not much is changing, this is just about tolerable (though not very motivating), but in the complex and dynamic marketplaces we find ourselves in, it becomes imperative for everyone to have defined objectives. When targets are not clear, people make them up. And some seize upon the opportunity to redefine the goals to suit their own purposes. Managers are well placed to empire-build, and conflicts can easily arise between departments.

Complex structures: 'Who is supposed to do what?'

Any organizational structure that creates ambiguity or dual accountability is likely also to provoke a higher level of political activity – both constructive and destructive – purely because of the set-up. Over the years, matrix structures have become increasingly popular, but there has been little real effort made to ensure that they work in practice. People find themselves with two bosses – or even three or more – with the associated threat of disagreement between the parties in power. There is also, of course, a risk of ambiguity. As a consequence, it is common to find individuals vying for power and influence. When structures are complex, success requires a great deal of negotiation and cooperation – and a real ability to reconcile differing requests and priorities.

No clear definition of performance: 'What makes for success?'

Linked with this, politicking will be high when it's unclear what you need to do to get on – or even to get a good appraisal. When the process lacks objectivity, people are left with little choice but to trumpet their own successes and play down the contribution of others. Boss management also becomes important; investing time in ingratiating yourself with your boss – and your boss's bosses – can pay dividends. And making sure that you don't get blamed for any failures is key. At the beginning of the financial crisis, one global investment bank declared that – in the difficult circumstances – it intended to ditch its established performance management process. No longer would colleagues be invited to give feedback about one another. Review of progress against objectives would be put on hold for the year and evaluation of an individual's contribution would be left to their manager's discretion. And the effect of this? Negative politicking went through the roof. Some people opted out altogether. Morale dipped even further. Many found themselves victims of their more unscrupulous colleagues. And if people disagreed with the way in which they had been recognized and rewarded, there was very little they could do about it.

Transparent remuneration and reward systems, along with honest and clear career planning, are critical in reducing negative politicking of this kind and ensuring that your business is a genuine meritocracy.

High level of change: 'What's going on?'

In the first decade of this millennium, we have witnessed unprecedented levels of change – and change can cause fear, uncertainty and ambiguity. No one has been untouched by the global financial crisis – whether as an employee or as a citizen – and this is probably the single biggest contributor to the increase in politics, as witnessed by 60 per cent of our respondents. Interestingly, at the height of the crisis, that number was higher than 90 per cent; as the world tries to make sense of what has happened, and the course becomes increasingly clear, there is a corresponding fall in the perceived levels of politicking. It's still high, however, and savvy is still a critical skill at work.

Refusal by powerful people to change: 'Why aren't they role modelling this?'

The behaviour of people in senior positions has a massively disproportionate effect on the workforce; people hang on their every word – and action – watching carefully for hidden meaning. Messages are scrutinized and mistakes jumped on. The observers might be looking to follow a lead, or merely to criticize the leadership. Either way, it can become quite obsessive. And when people in influential positions refuse to toe the corporate line, this can spark political battles throughout the organization. People complain of lip service and hypocrisy. They sneer at the corporate values as works of fiction. And, as we observed earlier, this can cause rivalry between different teams, destructive game playing in the boardroom and a cynical, demoralized workforce.

Punishment culture: 'Why blame me?'

When the organization is tough on poor performers, or likes to publicize failures as a warning to others, it becomes very important for people to cover their tracks carefully and ensure that nothing that does go wrong can be traced back to them. E-mail becomes an essential tool; those who are most adept at avoiding blame are usually also firm believers in the 'audit trail'. They anticipate likely problems and cover their tracks with e-mails, copied and blind copied, as necessary, which clearly demonstrate that they are in the clear. When this strategy fails – as it inevitably does, from time to time – these people will have convincing scapegoats at the ready. Punishment cultures provide fertile breeding ground for political animals.

Limited resources: 'How can we be expected to deliver this?'

When teams have to compete for headcount and budget, they will need to exert political influence in order to ensure that their work is regarded as an organizational priority.

Jobs at risk: 'Why us?'

At the time of writing, over 6 million jobs have been lost in the United States since President Obama took office. In the UK, unemployment is at its highest for 17 years – more than a million amongst 16- to 24-year-olds, for the first time. People are therefore fearful that they will be out of work and need to protect themselves. By their own admission, they may engage in activities that they wouldn't normally feel comfortable with – and some of this is negative politicking.

Remember, people can use the phrase 'office politics' glibly, as shorthand for dissatisfaction. They're often surprised by the level of 'politicking' that goes on inside companies, but what they're describing is the inevitable effect of operating in an organizational environment – with conflicting objectives, clashing priorities, different styles and the operation of both formal and informal mechanisms. It's important to view the situation as objectively as you possibly can, and to examine your position and your interpretation of events. A field manager of a large manufacturing company, promoted to head office, could not believe the degree of office politics – but actually, he just wasn't used to it. What he was describing was corporate reality, and what he needed to do was to learn to live in it, proactively, productively and without becoming a victim.

So what is savvy?

What then are the skills required to deal with the politics – both positive and negative? What is entailed in being savvy? In the words of some of the people who participated in our 2011 survey, the skills and behaviours include:

- 'Influencing and relationship development – and navigating your way through those different layers and levels. I'm mindful of who the decision makers, the key influencers and the stakeholders are.'
- 'Knowing who pulls the strings, avoiding treading on others' toes and keeping people onside.'
- 'Identifying allies and foes.'
- 'Understanding the context, the differing agendas and different personalities that people in the organization have.'
- 'Keeping your eyes open and actively listening. Then asking good questions.'
- 'Demonstrating emotional intelligence.'
- 'Being clued up about what motivates others.'
- 'Understanding the interrelationships of others, in terms of the camps and alliances.'
- 'Reconciling differences.'

- 'Enhancing your profile and your position, and making sure that people know what to come to you for.'

- 'Being on others' radars for the right reasons.'

- 'Having an appreciation of the context and rationale, so you know why decisions are being made – and what the decision-making process is.'

- 'Being aware of what the politics are, so that you can then choose whether to play or not.'

- 'Using your judgement to ensure you employ appropriate behaviour to reach the right outcome.'

- 'Not using the politics as a tool to the detriment of others.'

Going back to the definition at the start of this chapter, an individual who demonstrates savvy is someone who understands and utilizes the dynamics of power, organization, and decision making to achieve objectives.

Summary

So, in summary, office politics can be defined as the informal, rather than the formal, way of getting things done. We also need to bear in mind that politicking can be both constructive and destructive. When motives are pure, when methods are confined within the limits of reasonable behaviour and the company's performance is on the up, then office politics may not be too distracting or damaging. It's also likely that the incidence of political behaviour in the office will be kept to a minimum – because it's simply not needed. It's where the opposite of these conditions prevails that office politics gains its unsavoury reputation.

People who demonstrate political savvy, then, are those who know where the power lies, understand how to obtain it for themselves and others, and possess the skills to use it in the pursuance of common goals. This is constructive when the individual is seeking success for the organization or team, but it can become destructive when this motivation is selfish or unethical, or if unacceptable methods are employed to achieve the individual's ambitions.

Chapter Two
Adopting a positive, proactive approach

> If you think you can, or you think you can't,
> you're probably right!
>
> Mark Twain

The world is in a state of turmoil and flux, politically and financially. Economies are floundering, job losses are rife, and uncertainties are multiplying. At the same time, advances in technology and the way we do business are transforming the landscape. Organizations and people are having to make massive adjustments and the ultimate impact of all this change is still unknown. Across the globe, people complain that there's no chance to embed any of the changes and they are realistic enough to know that there's little possibility of things settling down. Ambiguity, complexity and the fast pace of change are here to stay. This is fertile ground for office politics, and the type of conditions in which the office politicians thrive.

So how do you respond? Do you put your head down, pretend nothing's happening and hope for the best? Or do you approach events with your eyes wide open and try to make a difference where you can? Do you complain about how unfair and hopeless everything is, or do you assume responsibility for putting matters right? One thing's for sure – you can't be savvy unless you are proactive and positive.

Are you a victim?

During a discussion about influencing internal customers, a middle manager in an accounts department was heard to say: 'Influencing is not relevant in our job. We can't influence. We have no authority at all. All the people we are dealing with are just ignoramuses. They don't give us what we need to do the job and we can do nothing about it.'

Clearly a victim. But not only was this individual limiting her own impact, she was also setting a really bad example for her team, who – unsurprisingly – also adopted this negative, whinge-ing approach. Are you a victim of the politics? How exposed are you right now? You may not be quite so downbeat as this accounts manager, but there may be more subtle ways in which you find yourself on the receiving end, instead of being in the driving seat. Use the checklist in Figure 2.1 to assess whether destructive politics is affecting you.

FIGURE 2.1

 1 You find out what others are saying about you from third parties. ☐

 2 You can't really trust people. ☐

 3 People who get on are not necessarily the most deserving. ☐

 4 People are quick to point the finger when something goes wrong. ☐

 5 There are lots of cliques and you don't seem to be part of them. ☐

 6 There are lots of informal meetings in rooms with closed doors. ☐

 7 Colleagues talk about others behind their backs. ☐

 8 People tend to be suspicious about decisions taken. ☐

 9 People are suspicious of others' motives. ☐

10 Gossip is rife. ☐

11 You believe that others take the credit for your successes. ☐

12 You are pressurized into doing favours for others. ☐

13 People seem to be grabbing as much turf as they can. ☐

Thirteen ticks would be very unlucky indeed! But if you have experienced any in your recent working life, it would make sense to examine why this is happening and what it might be symptomatic of. The guidelines later in this book will enable you to adopt a proactive approach, to help you to recognize office politics at work, confront any issues raised, and generally enhance your powers of influence. But you will first need to understand why you have been a victim. There are many possible reasons, but do any of the following sound familiar?

- 'There's nothing I can do.'
- 'I never see it coming.'
- 'I can't be bothered.'
- 'I don't know how.'

'There's nothing I can do'

Think about the people in your organization. How many of them truly make a difference? Or more to the point, how many of them make *as much* difference as they could do if they really put their mind to it? The answer is probably depressing. It's a fact of life that it's easier to criticize others' actions and complain about the sorry state of affairs than it is to do something about it. Not only is it easier, but if we're honest with ourselves, it's more fun too. Gossiping and a good group moan have a sort of therapeutic effect – changing the situation requires hard graft, individuality, the ability to bounce back from setbacks, and unquenchable optimism!

Then there are the people, verging on the paranoid, who are convinced that this kind of thing only ever happens to them; others really do have it in for them. And they firmly believe that the resolution is outside their control – someone else will have to sort it out if, indeed, it's possible to solve the problem.

Both these responses are reactive approaches. They are typical of people who don't really make a difference – or, at least, don't make the positive difference they should.

To what extent does this describe you? Do you complain rather than challenge? Are you good at finding a hundred reasons why you can't do something rather than getting on with it? Do you shy at the first hurdle rather than finding a way to soar effort-lessly over it? Or are you the sort of person who does take control and influence the situation where you can? You can see where you stand on this by considering the 10 short questions below. Answer yes or no to each, depending on which more accurately represents your situation or view.

1 Is there some habit, such as smoking, that you'd like to break but can't?

2 Do you feel your own personality was laid down firmly by childhood experiences, so that there is little you can do to change it?

3 Do others seem to get all the breaks?

4 Do you find it a waste of time planning ahead, because something always seems to turn up to change your plans?

5 Do you find it difficult to say 'no' to people?

6 Do you find yourself procrastinating and putting things off?

7 Do you often feel you are the victim of forces outside your control?

8 Do you find that other people usually get their way?

9 Do you wait for the phone to ring and then feel rejected when it doesn't?

10 Would your friends and colleagues like you to take more responsibility for things?

The more affirmative answers you have given to these questions, the more likely it is that you are a *reactive* rather than a *proactive* person; you let things happen to you rather than influencing situations and taking control. But even if your answers do place you in this category, does it really matter? The short answer is almost certainly yes. As well as having less impact, reactive people are more likely to feel oppressed by the flow of events; in extreme cases, they are prone to free-floating anxiety (worry without a specific cause) and often feel like running away. They can even make themselves ill: the condition known as 'learned helplessness' – identified by American psychologist Professor Martin Seligman – is a recognized symptom of clinical depression. It is characterized by the feeling that, whatever you do, it won't make a difference. People who feel this way are more likely to be victims of bullies and destructive office politicians, who are rarely inclined to pick on stronger, more assertive people. Less drastically, reactive people are often considered to be energy sapping, because of their apparent lack of drive – and constant complaining.

But reactive people aren't always the shrinking-violet type. There are also the people who could be described as 'passive aggressives'. Yes, they make their voices heard; yes, you know they're unhappy with the situation. But what they rarely focus on is actions that *they* could take to make a positive difference.

Genuinely proactive people do make things happen – in a way that seems well suited to the situation. These are the people we tend to admire – the winners. They're the ones who work themselves into the best jobs, are full of self-confidence, appear to be on top of things and seem able to deal with anything that life throws at them. Of course, they run the risk of being envied rather than admired by those less assured than themselves, but they are usually judged to be a positive influence and stimulating companions.

Stephen Covey, in his book *The 7 Habits of Highly Effective People*, talked about a circle of concern and a circle of influence. The circle of concern holds everything that you might worry, or even think, about. Within this is a subset – the circle of influence – which contains those issues over which you can have some direct influence or control. Since you only have a finite number of hours in the day, and limited energy, it makes sense to focus your attention on those things you can impact upon positively. If you fail to do this, you inevitably shrink your circle of influence, resulting in a 'reactive' focus.

You can teach yourself to be more proactive by reframing your thinking. Conceptually, this is a simple technique, involving three stages:

1 Be in tune with your thinking.

2 Recognize when it is negative and reactive.

3 Turn this thinking around, so that it is more positive and proactive.

So, if you find yourself thinking 'There's nothing I can do,' the reframe might be 'Of course there's something I can do. Let me make a list of the key stakeholders and work out how I can try to influence each one.'

As with many of these techniques, it is simple to describe but much more difficult to put into practice. It requires determination and discipline. But it is a fact that someone who naturally errs on the reactive side can reverse this tendency by using this simple technique.

'I never see it coming'

Some people appear to have the ability to see round corners – and over the horizon. They are exceptionally talented at anticipating difficulties. They know what's coming. Others are not only taken by surprise but they also seem to make the same mistakes time and time again. They don't learn from problems that have arisen in the past – and so are likely to become victims of negative politicking. To minimize this risk, it is vital to be astute. You need to be aware of what's going on around you, think through why others might be behaving in the way they are, and invest time in anticipating consequences. You must also be able to spot the flags. But what are these situations that you need to be alert to? The list is endless, but includes:

- when you are removed – from a project team, a regular meeting, a circulation list;

- when someone's behaviour changes towards you – they might become more aggressive or just start to ignore you;

- when lots of meetings are taking place behind closed doors;

- when you are hearing mixed messages;

- when you are pumped for information but you don't know why;

- when you are asked for input but not invited to be involved or don't have your name attached to the work;

- when others around you appear to be sucking up to the boss;

- when your boss seems to lose credibility or respect in the business;

- when you hear things that others have said about you rather than to your face.

This list is not exhaustive. In one investment bank, we asked a group to list the situations they thought people needed to look out for. They rapidly identified over 100.

Interestingly, it is often an afterthought that individuals also need to watch for flags as *perpetrators* of a political situation

– not just as victims. Everyone, at some point or another, does something that causes a problem. What might that be? What happens when you:

- fail to get input from key stakeholders?
- forget to inform people who have an interest in what you're doing – no matter how tenuous?
- are indiscreet or disparaging about others?
- demonstrate favouritism, no matter how subtly?
- push 'send' on an inappropriate e-mail?
- have sent an e-mail to the wrong people?
- are overly direct – or not direct enough?
- are cowardly and don't deal with situations, allowing them to snowball?
- are a poor role model?

Each of these actions might result in a difficult political situation. Sometimes even the most innocent act – or omission – can trigger a chain of events, with catastrophic consequences. Stopping for a moment to consider the possible effects of what we are about to do or say would help to minimize this risk.

There's a fine line, however, between being alert to what's going on and being paranoid. It wouldn't do at all for you to walk in the door in the morning with a constant stream of anxiety-provoking questions running through your mind: 'Why did he do that?' 'What could she mean by paying me that compliment?' 'Can I really believe what he just said?' 'Why is she smiling; what's behind that?' It's important to be in tune with your surroundings and connected with other people. It also makes sense to check out the concerns spawned by sensitive scrutiny of what is going on around you. But be on the lookout for a visit from Captain Paranoia – and remember you have a job to do!

'*I can't be bothered*'

You may find yourself the victim of political operators because you choose not to engage. You might be fully aware of what's coming down the line, but you don't have the time or the inclination to deal with the problems. Perhaps you're exhausted – you've already worked a 10-hour day – or you've got a spreadsheet to finish. In our recent survey on political savvy, 65 per cent of people admitted that they couldn't be bothered with playing politics. Since the same survey revealed that three-quarters consider political savvy to be critical in developing their career, it's clear that many people seem bent on limiting their own potential.

Interestingly, when this situation is probed, it usually emerges that people who feel this way do so very strongly. It's frequently not just a question of not having time, but these individuals have a real issue with *why they should*. They say things like 'Surely my results speak for themselves. I don't know why I should have to do all these additional things.' This is often followed by 'I feel very uncomfortable blowing my own trumpet.' And when pressed further, they will often get to 'This is just wrong and it's not me.' For them, possessing political savvy is somehow akin to behaving badly, or even unethically.

Is this how you feel? If so – and if you do want to develop your political savvy – a vital step is to shift your view of office politics. Earlier in the chapter, we mentioned reframing. This technique could help you to develop a more positive perception of political savvy. Furthermore, it might be useful for you to think about the consequences of your reluctance to engage. If you don't publicize your successes and the successes of the team, people are unlikely to be aware of your excellent work. Could you be accused of failing to share good news and best practice? And is there a risk that the team will suffer when it comes to recognition and reward? If you don't communicate as widely – and as effectively – as you can, will others feel out of the loop and become more likely to resist your ideas? If you don't actively influence the powers that be, you can't really complain when your projects fail through lack of support. Unfortunately, such considerations often aren't enough to persuade the most reluctant office politicians that the benefits of engaging outweigh what they perceive to be an affront to one of their core values. A vital consideration for such people is how they can engage with the politics in a way which doesn't offend their personal integrity.

'I don't know how'

Suppose you've decided to take a positive proactive approach and have learned how to read situations, but you still don't know what to do when difficult situations come along. If this is the case, the remainder of this book will help you to enhance your political savvy. It strongly advocates a positive, proactive approach, whether you are dealing with a perceived injustice or merely ensuring that your powers of influence and persuasion are up to scratch. It will not turn you into what others would describe as a political animal. Instead it's all about coping and dealing constructively with issues, making sure that you aren't a victim of destructive office politics – either of your own making or at the hands of others. The book is for anyone who works in a company – at whatever level and in whatever industry. It works on the basis that, in business life, you have two types of situation to deal with: overcoming challenges and exploiting opportunities.

Chapter Three
Who is savvy?

> Man is by nature a political animal.
>
> Aristotle, *Politics*

Research findings have always been clear-cut: the most successful people tend to be politically adept. They understand that all organizations are political systems. Perhaps more importantly, they know how to work them: if you want to get funding, influence others, win people over in conflict situations, get recognition for what you've done and ultimately get on, you need to be politically savvy. And this has never been the case more than it is now.

Since most people acknowledge that the politics are everywhere – and they also (some grudgingly) recognize the need to be politically savvy – it's surprising that the term *office politics* continues to have negative connotations. More often than not, it's still a label reserved for behaviours which are underhand, manipulative or damaging to others. But it's clear that there are people who play the politics constructively. What's the difference? Well, it's a question of not just *what* you're doing, but also *why* you're doing it: your motives and your methods. To distinguish between negative, destructive politicking and positive, constructive politicking, you need to explore both dimensions.

Your methods

This describes how well you handle situations. Do you know the right people, understand where the power lies, influence effectively and achieve success – regardless of how 'success' is defined? If so, you will score highly in terms of your methods. By contrast, if you are rather clumsy in your communication, struggle to get others to do what you want them to do and rub people up the wrong way, you will score negatively.

Your motives

More important, however, are your motives. To score highly on this scale, you need to have the organization's and your team's interests at heart. You believe passionately that your preferred course of action is the right thing to do. You act in the pursuance of the greater good. On the other hand, if your motives are selfish, or even vindictive, this sits firmly in the negative category.

Your savvy

In short, 'methods' relate to the ability of the individual to understand and play the politics of an organization, while the 'motives' axis is more concerned with why they would want to. Both are important and together they constitute savvy.

Who are the political players?

So the first step in demonstrating savvy involves understanding who you're dealing with. The combination of methods and

FIGURE 3.1

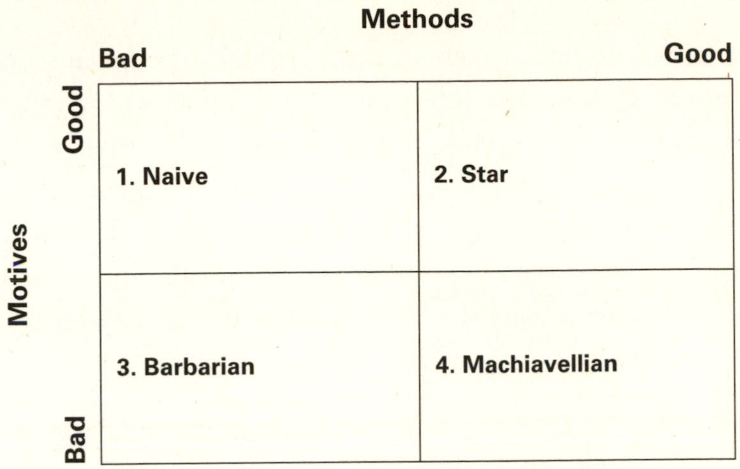

Methods

	Bad	**Good**
Good (Motives)	1. Naive	2. Star
Bad	3. Barbarian	4. Machiavellian

motives generates a number of different types of behaviour, of which the four principal characters are given in Figure 3.1.

Boxes 1 and 2 contain people who are driven by altruistic motives. Stars possess the political skill required to operate effectively in an organizational context. They are often both competent and admired, whereas Naives are well intentioned, but don't have the political skill to achieve their objectives. They may be perceived as irritants, innocents, militants or well-meaning incompetents.

In boxes 3 and 4 we have people who are driven by suspect motives – politicians in the most negative sense of the word. Even 450 years after its publication, Niccolò Machiavelli's tract *The Prince* remains the most chilling application of the belief that the end justifies the means. Frustrated by the constant political turbulence of the times he lived in, Machiavelli's advice to governments reflected his conviction that the political status quo must be protected at any cost. 'Machiavellian' therefore is the description reserved for those people, driven by 'bad' motives, who are adept at understanding and interpreting situations, and making happen what they want to happen.

Barbarians are more likely to be *described* as politicians, since their activities are less subtle and their motives easier to read. They may be prone to misjudging situations or acting in a way that is transparently self-seeking. They will criticize colleagues behind their backs and talk down the contribution of others. They certainly don't possess the political nous of the Machiavellian and are therefore less effective at making things happen – and at covering their tracks.

Let's look at some examples in business life. During the election process for a senior partner of a global professional services firm, one partner took it upon himself to campaign, informally, for one of the candidates. He did this believing that, if successful, the candidate would award him a significant position on the management board. They had had conversations alluding to this, but no concrete promises were made. Just before the election, the partner unearthed some information which was damaging to the candidate's main rival and so selectively leaked this. Inevitably, the information became public knowledge and the rival discredited. The campaign was a 'success'. Once in post, however, the newly appointed senior partner failed to honour his part of the unwritten agreement; he did not allocate a managerial role to the partner who had worked so hard on his behalf. But the partner couldn't say anything, since to do so would mean confessing to some unacceptable behaviour. In this situation, it is probably fair to say that both belong in the bottom half of the matrix – but on which side?

And what about the chief executive of a large European construction company, who allowed a senior member of his executive team to remain in post, despite knowing that this individual was not only performing poorly but was also overly controlling and undermining of others? The chief executive was loyal to this team member – and was trying to protect him – but at the expense of others and of the business. The chief executive argued that his motives were well intentioned, but others – particularly those who reported directly to the failing director – criticized him for not grasping the nettle. So this man would sit somewhere on the left-hand side of the matrix.

We have also encountered a number of quite senior managers who indulge in negative politics purely because they *enjoy* it. They are people who get a kick out of playing one person off against another. They consider it a matter of personal honour to beat an internal rival – whether it's in the company's interests or not. They delight in making others squirm by exploiting difficult interpersonal dynamics. For them, a day in the office is not complete without some good political fun. Bad motives again.

You may be able to spot people like that, but are they able to spot themselves? How many people have you ever heard own up to this kind of behaviour? And these examples raise an interesting aspect of the politics: what appear to be positive, well intentioned motivations to the architect can be interpreted very differently by others. And it's striking how effective such individuals can be at justifying their actions. Powerful and articulate leaders are often adept at positioning manipulative and self-serving actions as being in the best interests of the company, consumers or even the community as a whole.

Being savvy, then, has many aspects. You need to ensure that your actions are above board and that, hand on heart, your motives are pure. In addition, it will inevitably involve confronting behaviours that you don't believe to be constructive or ethical on the part of others. The ability to distinguish between constructive and destructive politics is vital.

In our 2011 survey, 56 per cent of all respondents describe themselves as being politically savvy. And an encouraging 70 per cent of people believe that their colleagues have positive motives. A generation of Stars perhaps? In contrast to these positive perceptions, in the prior 12 months, half of the respondents said they'd had someone else take the credit for their work, 37 per cent had witnessed bullying, over a quarter lamented the fact that their colleagues don't keep their promises, and almost 40 per cent complained about the fact that they'd discovered others had been criticizing them behind their backs. Not well intentioned, you might argue. More worryingly, 14 per cent observed that the structure of remuneration packages encourages people to act unethically, 9 per cent said it's OK to act unethically if there's enough at stake, and 11 per cent admitted to knowingly leaking information – all behaviours which are more indicative of a Machiavellian or a Barbarian.

Why do people behave in a negative way?

Why do some behave in a Machiavellian or Barbarian fashion? Well, why do people do anything bad? There is always a variety of reasons, many of which will never be truly understood by a third party – and some of which may well be unknown to the perpetrator; the subconscious mind has a lot to answer for! But let's talk about some of the obvious ones: greed, insecurity, envy, arrogance, cowardice, and revenge.

The first of these, and perhaps the most relevant in the present context, is greed. You could argue that greed was largely to blame for the global financial crisis. The stories of excess and extravagance are well documented. But it's not just bankers whose behaviours can take a turn for the worse when large sums of money are at stake. Take the scandal of politicians' expenses in the UK. Taxpayers' money was spent illicitly on a range of goods and services. Some were silly. Some downright unlawful. A number of politicians claimed for mortgage payments when their debts had already been repaid some years earlier. They lied about where they lived to exploit the system and claimed for journeys that had never been taken. There were £8,000 televisions, massage chairs, duck houses, antique rugs, new kitchens – the list goes on. But it's not just money that can provoke greed. People might be hungry for power, status and success – or a colleague's job – which can lead to excessively competitive behaviour and dirty dealing. Greed has a lot to answer for.

Insecurity is another matter. It is reasonable for people to feel insecure in turbulent market conditions. They fear for their jobs and for their livelihoods. But for some people, insecurity has been a lifelong curse. The causes are many: difficult childhoods, unfavourable comparisons, perceived failures – the list is endless. But the result is often the same: low self-esteem, which breeds insecurity. This, in itself, is no crime! Many people who are lacking in self-confidence are perfectly charming and behave immaculately. But it can also lead to negative motives and underhand methods – putting other people down, for instance, failing to acknowledge their contribution, or even telling lies about them. These are all examples of insecurity-fuelled politicking.

Linked to this is envy. People want what others have – or at least would prefer it if the other person's talents were rated less. Often *driven* by insecurity, envy takes many forms. It might be a boss who knows that a direct report is more gifted than they are. Or an individual who is jealous of a colleague's popularity. Or a feeling that someone else always gets the best work and has the easiest time. Those who envy others fail to recognize that people generally make their own luck, and are loath to admit that the objects of their envy often deserve what they get.

And the result? Our research flagged up some shocking examples of what can happen when people are jealous. Like the senior director who wanted to move his family back home from another continent and set his heart on a female colleague's job. She wasn't going anywhere, so he embarked upon a campaign to undermine her performance and discredit her.

Arrogance is quite different. Fuelled by extreme – and often unwarranted – self-belief, arrogance can convince people that they know better than anyone else. And the result? Arrogant people become autocratic. They rarely consult others and, when opposing views are voiced, they don't listen. This means they may fail to heed warning signs, sometimes with catastrophic consequences. Take Fred Goodwin. In the space of 10 years, he transformed RBS from a second-division regional bank into one of the biggest financial institutions in the world. Year after year he was voted Scotland's most powerful person. Perhaps he came to see himself as invincible. But former colleagues say that he became arrogant and, after the takeover of NatWest, few of RBS's acquisitions made sense. Performance tailed off, leading to the biggest public bail-out of a British bank – and Fred's sacking. As a leader, Fred apparently brooked no criticism and held extremely strong views.

Next on the list is cowardice. This implies a reluctance to grasp the nettle and deal with difficult issues. It usually arises in conflict situations, when it's necessary to deliver an unwelcome message, or when tough decisions have to be made. Ill feeling festers and performance deteriorates, often leading to a total breakdown of the situation. For instance, a chief executive who failed to deal with a personality clash between two directors on her team found the organization divided. Four directors walked out and the CEO faced a steep uphill struggle to rebuild morale. Her colleagues said that she had lacked the courage to deal with what was initially a simple issue.

Which leads us to revenge! It's a rare person who has never been made furious by someone or something at work: for many people it's a daily occurrence. For your average Machiavellian or Barbarian, it is then a matter of pride to wreak horrible revenge. This might involve spreading a rumour, forwarding a damaging e-mail, causing failure or reputational harm, or, in extreme circumstances, getting the other person fired.

Whilst a good starting point, this list is not exhaustive. Anything that causes bad behaviour in life has the potential to cause negative, destructive politicking in the workplace. We need to be alert to it, both in others and in ourselves; removing the cause will usually remedy the symptom!

How do you behave?

So you do need political savvy to survive and thrive in the corporate world – without it, you are unlikely to be sufficiently tuned in to know what to do and how to do it. But this is quite a different thing from the manipulation of events for selfish reasons, or taking pleasure from playing one person off against another. Motives and methods are all-important in determining which camp you fall into, so you need to challenge yourself on two fronts.

Challenge No.1: What *is* your motivation? *Why* are you playing the politics? Is it truly because you want the team to be successful or is it because you want to shine personally? Is it because it's the only way to get things moving or is it because you thrive on the game playing? Is it because you are protecting others or is it because you doubt your own ability and their success threatens you? Question your motives. Challenge yourself. Understand why you behave as you do. There's nothing wrong with a win–win situation, but if your success means

FIGURE 3.2

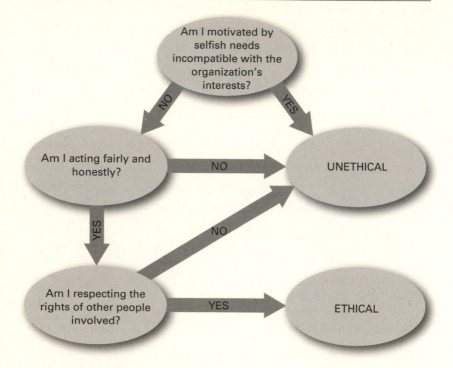

another's failure, what's the likely impact on them – and on others in the company? Every time you have a difficult decision to take, try the ethics test in Figure 3.2.

Challenge No. 2: It's equally important to think about the *way* you do things. There's a difference between influence and manipulation, as there is between constructively handling conflict and bullying. It's all in the manner in which you do it. Here too, you need to examine your own approach. Be honest. Are there things you do that you're not proud of? Do you feel that you could be more effective if you modified your style in some way?

The appendix to this book contains a quiz, which will enable you to assess your own political savvy and determine how close you are to being a star. Better still, you can log on to

www.officepoliticssurvey.com and have your personalized report e-mailed to you. In under 10 minutes, you will be able to assess your own political savvy *and* offer your views on the office politics in your world. But be honest – if you cheat, you'll only be deceiving yourself! Whatever your response, this book is focused on helping you become more of a Star at work.

To end ...

The former British Labour politician Lord (Peter) Mandelson, a political 'fixer' par excellence sometimes referred to as the Prince of Darkness, was asked about his favourite political books. His list included *The Prince* by Niccolò Machiavelli, which he apparently dips into from time to time. For what, advice? In his time, Machiavelli has been likened to Satan – and Satan to Machiavelli. And Machiavelli's words are certainly chilling. For example, he proposes that it is better to kill a man's father than to steal his inheritance, on the basis that the death of a father will soon be forgotten whilst the theft will be remembered and avenged for generations. Less brutally, he observes that – if you can't be both – it is safer to be feared than to be loved. And famously, he talked about the end justifying the means. It is difficult to tell, however, the extent to which he advocated the principles outlined in *The Prince* or whether he was merely observing and reporting how best to secure and retain power.

Chapter Four
Dealing with the office politicians

> It is said that if you know your enemies and know yourself, you will not be imperilled in a hundred battles; if you do not know your enemies but do know yourself, you will win one and lose one; if you do not know your enemies nor yourself, you will be imperilled in every single battle.
>
> Sun Tzu, *The Art Of War*

Despite everything we said in Chapter 3 'Who is savvy?' it is important to remember that situations, as well as personalities, drive behaviour. So you should try to avoid pigeonholing people, unless you have really good reason to do so. Just because you found out that a colleague not only claimed credit for your work but has also been criticizing your contribution to anyone who will listen, that doesn't necessarily make them a Barbarian. They have done it once, and they may well believe that they had good cause to act in the way they did. From your perspective, their motives are negative and, since you've found out what they've done, the chances are their methods haven't been that effective either. But perhaps it's a one-off. Wait until you catch them doing it again – to you or to others – or prove themselves to be untrustworthy in other ways, before writing them off as a Barbarian.

Similarly, Naive – or even militant – behaviour might be merely the result of a very bad day and a dose of fatigue. It doesn't mean to say that the individual will always act like a bull in a china shop. As for the Machiavellian, it could just be that they have a different agenda from yours; they see things differently. And even the Stars can slip up. They might find themselves caught unawares or completely at a loss as to how to deal with a tricky issue.

So until you know someone better, treat each situation on its merits and suspend judgement. Once you are convinced, however, that the person fits into a particular category, you will then need to be savvy in terms of how you handle them. In this chapter, we provide some general principles and then dedicate a section to each of the main characters, with some views as to how you spot them and deal with them.

General principles

Much of the advice about dealing with others in difficult situations comes down to being alert and mindful rather than just blundering in! As soon as you are aware of a problem, take a moment to examine the situation from all perspectives. Analyse your own motives and try hard to understand the other party's, putting yourself firmly into their shoes. What do they want? Why are they behaving in this manner? What's driving them? Read between the lines and try to understand the subtext. If this doesn't come naturally, examine the clues. Be honest with yourself. Quite often, we ignore strong signals when they don't support our own line. So what might you have overlooked or dismissed?

Having scrutinized the circumstances, you might still be none the wiser. Or you could lack confidence in the conclusions you've drawn. So it may make sense to talk to someone else.

Clearly, if you are going to turn to another, it is critical that they are trustworthy. Furthermore, they need to understand the confidentiality of the situation and the fact that you don't intend talking to anyone else about it – they are your confidential sounding board.

Explore the situation with them. Test out alternative approaches. Whatever course of action you ultimately decide to take, think through both the intended and the unintended consequences. Ensure that the resolution is worth the effort. Might it be better just to let it go this time?

Dealing with a Barbarian

Utter Barbarians have one redeeming feature: it's easy to spot them! They are constantly belittling others whilst talking them-selves up. They are kings and queens of the backhanded compli-ment. They are undermining of their colleagues and even, at times, bullying. And they do it in such an obvious way. When asked to describe a Barbarian, people often use words like 'obsequious', 'slimy', 'arrogant', 'devious', 'dishonest' and 'blunder-ing'. They might also mention the fact that many Barbarians come across as being deeply insecure, desperate to be seen as better than their peers but frequently achieving the opposite.

Behaviours to watch for when Barbarian-spotting include:

- gossiping behind colleagues' backs;
- very obviously trying to manipulate situations and people, but without much success;
- writing incriminating e-mails, often copying and blind copying others;
- trumpeting their own successes, with never a mention of the team;

- blaming team members when things go wrong;
- inappropriate or offensive language;
- sucking up to the boss;
- defensive aggression;
- displays of anger.

It's also interesting to observe how others behave in their company. They might refuse to listen, or roll their eyeballs when the Barbarian speaks.

Clearly, given the description above, the best way to deal with Barbarians is to avoid them; why on earth would you give yourself the headache of working with someone who displays these kinds of behaviours if you didn't have to? Besides which, you wouldn't want your reputation to be tarnished by association. However, it's not always possible to steer clear of them. You may need to deal with them on a daily basis. Or, perish the thought, you might even report to one of them! So if you can't keep away from them, the next best thing is to try to change them. Barbaric behaviour is not necessarily a life sentence. It may be possible to give them some feedback, pointing out the impact of their actions – on you, on others and on their reputation. You might also suggest what you suspect lies behind that behaviour. In other words, tell them what you think about their motives. This is, of course, a brave step, which could backfire on you. But even when it does, the chances are that others will recognize your positive motives and will back you.

Assuming that you can't, or won't, do either of these things, you need to develop strategies for making sure that you don't become a victim of the Barbarian's behaviour.

So, first and foremost, don't trust them. They're not trustworthy. If you confide in them, they will reveal your secret the moment the opportunity presents itself if they feel they can gain something from doing so – even if the benefit is just to ingratiate themselves with someone else. Nor will they back you. They demonstrate no loyalty, except to themselves, they will readily lay the blame at your door and will happily do a U-turn if they feel it will benefit their own cause. And they have no qualms about lying. No matter how trusting you are by nature, you need to be wary of the Barbarian.

It is also vitally important that you are strong and assertive with them. Many Barbarians are fundamentally insecure; they are also prone to bullying others. If you stand up to them, you are less likely to become a victim. Be careful not to let them drag you down to their level of behaviour. They have had much more experience at operating here, and will be able to make this experience count. Instead, you should insist on proprieties being observed.

Depending on the relationship you have with the Barbarian, there is a risk that you will be associated with them, and perhaps even tarred with the same brush. If this is the case, you need to avoid being seen to be allied to them, but without overtly criticizing. Find ways of demonstrating to other people how positive and competent you are. Identify the key players in your area and do whatever you can to forge strong, positive relationships with them. This could involve some lateral thinking on your part, but it's usually possible to find a reason to talk to and be supportive of others. And, when you're in meetings with a Barbarian, you may need to challenge some of their points – in a diplomatic way, of course!

E-mail is a challenging area when it comes to the Barbarian. They will forward, copy and misrepresent any e-mail sent by you if they can gain something by doing so. The rule of thumb, therefore, is to avoid getting into any e-mail exchange with them unless the subject matter is totally safe. You will, however, need to confirm, in writing, your understanding of every agreement you have with a Barbarian. Outline exactly who's doing what, what the next steps are and target deadlines. A failure to do this is likely to cause issues later on when the Barbarian flatly denies what you think has been agreed.

On the subject of tasks delegated to you by a Barbarian, it is very important that you ask a large number of questions to clarify the brief – especially why the work is being done in the first place, who commissioned it and who needs to see the results. Try to ensure that you feel fully comfortable with what's being demanded (remembering that you can't trust the Barbarian) and, if you're not, see if you can find an alternative way of achieving the objectives – one which you are OK with.

CASE STUDY

Josh was required to work with Adam to organize and run a series of client seminars in the United States. In Josh's view, Adam was the archetypal Barbarian – didn't do anything, was always thrashing around trying to find someone to blame, whilst claiming the credit when things did go well (largely due to the efforts of others). Having been on the receiving end of this behaviour on a number of occasions, Josh was concerned that his own reputation was starting to be damaged. He started to write very detailed e-mails, spelling out which activities were whose responsibility – making sure that they contained nothing that Adam could argue with. Being a Barbarian rather than a Machiavellian, Adam didn't read the signals. He continued to fail to deliver. Josh now had evidence. He wrote an e-mail to Adam, which was clear, calm and factual, attaching his previous messages and asking Adam why he had not delivered on his actions. Adam wrote one back, which merely contained three words: 'Blah! Blah! Blah!' Josh had everything he needed to make a case against Adam and took it up with senior management.

Dealing with a Machiavellian

Whilst the Machiavellian's motives are every bit as negative as the Barbarian's, the problem is that they are so skilled in handling the politics that it's much more difficult to spot them. In fact, most people report that they often haven't realized that another person has Machiavellian tendencies until they have fallen prey to them on a number of occasions. That's when the penny drops. The Machiavellian's activities are much more subtle and they are adept at avoiding detection. Sometimes the other party might have a nagging suspicion of negative motivation, but there is frequently a strong inclination to give the Machiavellian the benefit of the doubt. This is one of the reasons why they get away with it for so long.

Clearly, if you have been the victim a few times, then you will know. But if not, what might you look for? Be alert when dealing with someone:

- whose status seems to outstrip their ability;
- who confides in you for reasons you can't understand;
- whose name is associated with all the most successful projects, though it's often difficult to identify any significant contribution they have made;
- who is happy to use underhand or dishonest methods to get the results required;
- who always manages to avoid blame and whose reputation is untarnished even after the biggest disasters;
- who somehow gets others to do things they clearly won't benefit from – and which may well do them harm;
- who spends more time networking than doing;
- who seems to know everyone in power but doesn't bother with those who aren't.

Once you've identified a Machiavellian, knowing how to handle that person is a challenge. You're unlikely to be able to out-manoeuvre them, which leaves you with the following choices:

- accommodate them;
- exploit them;
- turn them;
- expose them.

Accommodation merely involves learning to live alongside the Machiavellian without compromising your own values and whilst minimizing the damage. Because their motives are similar to the Barbarian's, so too is some of the advice. So all the points about not trusting them, being careful with e-mails and asking lots of questions when they ask you to do something certainly apply – and even more so with the Machiavellian. When a Machiavellian starts to delegate a task to you, it is of critical importance to understand exactly what they are trying to achieve and why. Some of the following questions may be useful:

- Where has this come from?
- Why is it a priority now?
- Who's interested?
- Who else would be involved?
- How will you be involved?
- How much time is it likely to take?
- What are the critical outputs?
- What will happen to them?
- When are the deadlines?
- What are the risks involved?
- What are the likely benefits?

As you quiz them, you should convey an upbeat, constructive impression throughout, but try to avoid acquiescing prematurely, no matter how much pressure the Machiavellian applies. Master the art of sounding positive but without actually committing to doing what they want you to do. Of course, in the real world, you may well have no choice in the matter, but through questioning you can at least work out the extent of the possible damage and take action to minimize the risk.

As with Barbarians, you will benefit from being strong and assertive with the Machiavellian, not least since it will help your cause if they have some respect for you. And you must avoid showing any sign of weakness with them, no matter how tempting it is to be self-deprecating. If you do, they will take advantage of the knowledge or at least make sure that everyone else knows about your self-confessed 'failings'.

Beyond accommodation, you might decide to exploit the situation (but not, of course, the person!). Handled in the right way, you can use the Machiavellian's skills to help you to achieve your goals. You might build a carefully crafted relationship with them, which will enable you to gain access to their information and networks. Or, in certain situations, you can elicit their advice on how to handle a difficult issue. Be careful, though; it may make sense to check carefully any information gleaned from the Machiavellian to ensure that they're not selectively leaking to you. Furthermore, you will need to separate their motives from their methods. Don't forget that they're good at this stuff, but always be alert to tactics that appear devious or underhand.

But surely this approach is tantamount to becoming Machiavellian yourself? The answer to this question is 'no' – on the strict assumption that you are 100 per cent confident that your motives are legitimate and that your methods are above board.

Depending on your relationship with the Machiavellian and how hardened they are in their habits, it may be possible to turn them. This is, however, a high-risk strategy that will require careful planning on your part. As with the Barbarian, it will involve giving them feedback and flagging up the implications. There needs to be a really strong incentive for the Machiavellian to change, so you will need to think through what is likely to motivate them and how best to influence them. This is difficult enough if you are the person's manager, but if you report to them or they're a peer, it's nigh on impossible. In some instances, however, it might be worth a try; I can think of a couple of examples – but no more! – of Machiavellians turning into Stars.

The final strategy is to expose them. After all, if they are truly Machiavellian, their predominant driving force is self-seeking and their interests are often opposed to those of other people. They may be competitive internally, or vindictive, in ways which threaten the organization's smooth running. So it cannot be in the long-term interest of the organization to allow their behaviour to continue. Having said that, if you do plan to expose them, you need to do it carefully. First of all, think through exactly what you want to achieve. Would the best outcome be for them to leave or would you prefer the matter to be dealt with – and ideally rectified – by a senior manager? Absolute clarity of objective is key. The next stage is to gather evidence and to garner support, but you have to be sure that your allies are truly supportive. You need facts and you need people who are prepared to line up behind you. Those who have fallen victim to the Machiavellian's tendencies might be best placed to help.

Then determine who to talk to. This is likely to be someone in a position of power and potentially the Machiavellian's line manager – or their manager's manager. Remember, however, that Machiavellians are excellent at managing up and so this individual might have a wholly different perception of them from yours. If at all possible, avoid just tabling the problem; if you have thought through possible ways forward, this will help your message to land better.

Some HR departments provide a plausible alternative. HR people are bound by confidentiality but they also have an obligation to take some kind of action – should you wish them to. You may be able to talk through the situation, and the evidence, with them, and then seek their advice on how best to proceed. However, not all HR departments enjoy the kind of reputation that would encourage people to follow this course of action.

CASE STUDY

Alana had a Machiavellian boss. She didn't realize it at first: Philippe was always so positive, encouraging and, frankly, popular. But after a while, things started to go wrong for Alana. She found that, after she had been in a conversation with Philippe, she would feel less confident and somewhat troubled, but she couldn't put her finger on why. After a while, she came to dread their meetings, but they had one-to-ones every week and so she couldn't avoid him. And then matters got worse. Philippe would ask her to do things that clearly made her look stupid or incompetent. At one point, he appointed her as his deputy, but then reneged on the deal – but only after she'd turned up at a meeting to deputize for him, to be greeted by raised eyebrows and the chair of the meeting telling her that there must have been some mistake. Alana felt humiliated. She also found out much later on that Philippe had been sharing his 'worries' about her with senior stakeholders, and these concerns then came through in her feedback and appraisal. Whilst the criticisms were unjust, it was impossible to prove otherwise, and Alana's performance was perceived to have gone into decline. Alana tried to expose Philippe. She talked to HR about raising a grievance. Then she had a meeting with him, which was mediated by HR. All to no avail; Philippe did not feel bound by anything agreed at the meeting and did not uphold any of the actions. The turning point came during a conversation with her mentor – a senior and powerful director in another department. Alana had been pouring out her heart about Philippe to her mentor for many months, so he decided to take action. Exploiting his own power and status, the mentor took the issue to the top. After some enquiry, Philippe left the organization.

Dealing with a Naive

We have dealt with the characters who are consistently driven by negative motives. The Naives are wholly different. They absolutely do things for what they perceive to be the right reasons but they have a habit of handling situations ineffectively. It is therefore a lot easier to spot the Naive character by their tendency to:

- tell you that they can't be bothered playing the politics;
- believe that their good work will speak for itself and there should therefore be no need for self-promotion;
- indeed, feel that self-promotion is wrong;
- become a bit blinkered in their own work and, on occasion, fail to see the big picture;
- bemoan the fact that too much time is spent lobbying others for support, when it should just be clear-cut;
- send sharp e-mails;
- be overly direct;
- get passionate about issues, but not successfully influence others to effect a change;
- communicate on a 'need to know' basis.

Their heart may be in the right place and their motives beyond reproach, but they need to become a lot more effective before people will accept them as useful allies.

Since they are principled people, the first thing that you need to do with a Naive is to praise their integrity and make sure they know you are supportive of them. Once you have done this, it may be possible to give them a little feedback, focusing on the *implications* and *impact* of their behaviour. You will often find that – if you concentrate on how their actions might be detrimental to themselves – your feedback falls on deaf ears. They pride themselves on *not* being self-seeking. However, if you focus on potential damage to the team and others around them, you have a chance of engaging the Naive's interest.

Once you've gained their attention, you may want to steer the conversation towards what gets in the way. Why *aren't* they politically savvy? For some, their naive behaviour is caused by an inability to see things coming. They are frequently taken by surprise. In this case, helping them to get into the habit of anticipating potential problems and being more attuned to people and circumstances could be enough to address this. However, as we know, the Naive is often perfectly well aware of what's coming down the line, but they choose to ignore it and refuse to engage. At some level they think it's wrong and don't see why they should get sucked into the politics. This is the point at which you might need to get the Naive to reframe, encouraging them to view events more positively. It's not politicking, it's proactively influencing others. It's not blowing your own trumpet, it's ensuring that the team's successes are known and valued more widely. You might also draw their attention to the adverse consequences of not being savvy. But, whatever it takes, the Naive has to change their mindset about the politics.

It is only when they have become more willing to engage that you can think about helping them to be more able. If their outlook is blinkered, you'll want to get them to focus on the bigger picture. Looking at a wider network of stakeholders, pointing out how they could be interested in what the team is doing, and then agreeing how best to bring them into the fold are tactics that can work with the Naive. Or in conflict situations, you might help them to work out a strategy to resolve the problems. Encourage them to see things from others' points of view. Advise them on how they can refine their influencing skills. But, above all, steer them away from clumsy communication and ineffective militancy. Unlike the Machiavellian, the Naive can be seen as a Star-in-waiting; they merely need to hone their skills to move into this category, because their motivation is admirable.

CASE STUDY

Jo was a campaigner. Working for a charity, she was a staunch advocate of change. And she let everyone know. Jo prided herself on her straight talking and was convinced that her way was best. She was uninterested in 'playing the politics', preferring a much more direct approach. When she perceived that something wasn't being handled in the right way, or felt unjust, she would take it upon herself to let her managers know. It got to the point that they rather dreaded talking to her. Jo's heart was most certainly in the right place but her methods were ineffective. She just couldn't see it. So a close colleague took Jo to one side and gave her some detailed feedback. This focused largely on Jo's inability to get people on side – and how this had the effect of limiting her impact. The colleague had prepared for the conversation by gathering together a number of examples. Jo was terribly upset, but finally had to concede that her behaviour had been counterproductive; she was achieving the opposite effect to the one she desired. She immediately set about honing her skills of influence and persuasion. It was a long haul – much like unlearning the habits of a lifetime – but ultimately 'the cause' was more important to Jo than her own ego. She became an effective agent of change.

Dealing with a Star

It is interesting that Stars are not usually described as political. Instead, the words most frequently used to describe them include 'influential', 'a great leader', 'charismatic', 'a team player', 'practical', 'resourceful', 'well networked', 'problem solver', 'motivator', and so on. They are all the adjectives that we reserve for people who are successful and popular. They might also be described as being politically savvy, for that's what they are, though they are unlikely to describe themselves in this way.

So how do you handle the Stars? Some believe that you don't need to. Surely they're the ones managing situations and people, and ensuring that everyone's interests are, as far as possible, aligned. Why would other people need to handle them? Of course, this would not be the savvy response! Interaction with a Star provides a massive opportunity – to learn, to benefit and to support. By definition, helping to further the Star's cause is in the interest of the organization.

It stands to reason that you can gain the most from a Star if you have a good relationship with them. But to learn from them, you don't always have to. You can observe what they do from afar. And ask others about their approach. If you can get closer, do. Stars are excellent sounding boards when you have complex, thorny issues to deal with. Try not to use up your goodwill, though; don't turn to them every time something goes wrong. Save their help for the truly difficult issues. And remember to think things through for yourself before you approach them. You want to come across as being proactive and solutions orientated, even though you are seeking support.

If you have a strong relationship with a Star, you may be in the position to exploit a technique known as 'modelling'. This involves finding out not just what they do, but why they do it, and what's going through their minds as they do. First, identify a specific topic – something that they're particularly good at. Then come up with a list of questions: what do you want to know? Let's assume the topic is networking; the questions could be:

- What's your attitude towards networking?
- Has it always been that way?
- If not, how did you make the transition?
- How do you prepare for a networking event?
- What do you feel beforehand?
- What goes through your mind as you enter the room?
- What happens then?
- Do you enjoy it?
- What skills do you need to network well?
- What comes naturally to you?
- What is more difficult for you?
- How do you overcome difficulties?

Clearly, if you are going to ask a barrage of questions, it's important to get the Star's permission to run the exercise first. Position it as an experiment – a new tool that you'd like to try out.

We did this with a female partner in a law firm in front of a group of associates. She was a true Star, though she couldn't see it herself. The junior people were invited to quiz her about networking – with fascinating results. To their surprise, it turned out that the partner was not a natural networker at all. In fact, when she first had to attend large events, she was terrified. But she used her own experience and feelings to develop her skill. Instead of worrying about what other people would think about her – 'Why on earth would anyone be interested in me?' – she worked on the basis that there would be a significant number of people in the room who were experiencing the same feelings she was. When she first walked into the event, she would identify someone who was standing on their own – there was always at least one – and approach them immediately. With her opening questions prepared, she listened, was interested in the other person and demonstrated clear empathy for them. However, rather than stay with the same person for the duration, she drew others into the group and usually moved on, repeating the process. The key to her success was putting herself into the shoes of others instead of obsessing about how bad she felt. Not only did she become a comfortable networker, she was also a successful one. People remembered her interpersonal skills and her interest in others, which helped her to develop new business and her profile in the sector.

As well as learning from a Star, you may also be able to engage them to help you. Are there ways in which their support and involvement would be of benefit to what you're doing? If so, what specifically do you need from them? Would endorsement and sponsorship be sufficient – maybe just a word at the right time and place? Or do you need them to fulfil a more active role? Once you have established what you want, think about ways in which your objectives may also benefit the Star.

Reciprocity can be a useful tool. If you need the Star to support you, then it would make sense for you to think through how you can be of assistance to them.

When dealing with a Star, there is a series of balances that you need to strike:

- Convey a positive impression, but ...
- be honest and direct with them.
- Provide them with information, but ...
- don't gossip about others behind their backs.
- Seek their advice and input, but ...
- think through solutions for yourself first.
- Be respectful of their position and qualities, but ...
- make sure you come across as someone worth knowing, even if not quite their equal.
- Make a strong first impression, but ...
- build the relationship over time.

CASE STUDY

Eric felt he'd been handed the poisoned chalice; he was to lead a project to reorganize the department. Although it hadn't been said, it was clear that cuts were needed, so jobs were likely to be lost. Eric tried to push back, but he seemed to have no choice in the matter – he was to be the project manager. One of Eric's colleagues, Caroline, was perceived to be a Star. By rights, Eric felt she ought to be leading the project: she would surely know what to do and the most effective way to handle the sensitivities. However, she wasn't leading it. He decided that the next best thing would be to consult with and engage Caroline, seeking her input and advice. Wanting to come across as proactive, Eric documented the objectives and pulled together his thoughts about how best to proceed. He then asked her for a meeting. She was able to steer him not only in terms of the best plan of attack but also towards who to contact, how to get them on side and how best to communicate throughout the duration of the project. Eric took the bull by the horns and asked her to be actively involved. To his surprise, she agreed (preferring to be on the inside with an ability to influence the outcome) and became part of the project team. Eric ensured that he built a positive, powerful working relationship with her, which endured way beyond the project deadline. The project was still difficult, but the challenge was massively diminished by having Caroline alongside him.

Different people require different approaches. That much is clear. But if you are alert to a Star's behaviour, familiar with how they tend to react, and alert to their quirks and traits, you stand a much better chance of enlisting their support.

Chapter Five
Dealing with political problems at work

Craig's new product development (NPD) team operated in a global matrix. In other words, half the managers were responsible for regions and half for specific products. The regional people sat in the regions, close to the regional directors (RDs) but were still part of Craig's team, whilst the global people were situated centrally in New York. Things started to go wrong. The RDs were unhappy. They blamed the NPD team. The regional people were torn; they felt caught in the middle. They started to point the finger at their global colleagues. Tensions formed, but no one talked about their concerns face to face. Instead, a great deal was said behind colleagues' backs. Teamwork deteriorated. Trust broke down. Performance went into decline.

In the last chapter, we talked about how to handle particular character types. This advice will help you to demonstrate savvy when faced with negative politicking. It will also enable you to build relationships and learn from the Stars. However, this is only half the story. Knowing how to handle a Barbarian or a Machiavellian will help, but many of the people we've worked with over the course of the last decade have wanted to discuss how to deal with the specifics of individual, difficult circumstances too – regardless of who they're confronting. What *do* you do if there appears to be a smear campaign directed against you? Or if another individual consistently takes the credit for your work? The remaining chapters in this book contain a wealth of material on the general skills and behaviours that savvy people demonstrate. But, before getting into these, this chapter outlines the six most commonly experienced problems identified in our research, and explores each in detail – what causes it, why is it an issue and how can you solve it?

So what *are* the key issues? Our experience and research established that the six biggest problems (over and above the topics covered in the rest of this book) are as follows:

- being caught in the middle;
- someone stealing your credit;
- someone encroaching on your territory;
- being the victim of a smear campaign;
- dealing with hidden agendas;
- being held down.

There are, of course, a whole host of others, but if you can succeed in dealing with these, you will be equipped for much of the negative politicking that people say they face at work today.

Being caught in the middle

Being caught in the middle is one of the greatest problems in business today. Simply put, this is all about being asked to do two mutually contradictory things by two different people – or, in some instances, more! And over 70 per cent of respondents to our survey said that they had experienced this during the last year – significantly more for those aged under 30. Alternatively, you could be caught in the middle by being required to take sides in a conflict situation. This has always been an issue for people at work, but it has increased in recent years because of greater ambiguity, more complex structures – and the upsurge in negative politicking. This may be inevitable in uncertain times, but that's little comfort when you're the one caught in the middle. You might be damned either for not delivering or for delivering the wrong thing. The way in which others perceive your performance can be negatively impacted. If you're really unlucky, all parties might feel let down and turn on you. In the worst-case scenario, some people have even been asked to leave their organization merely because they have found themselves conflicted in this way.

CASE STUDY

Cara worked in HR. She was requested by a senior director in the business to head up a particular project for him – a development programme. Cara's boss, Louise, did not want her – or any of her peers – to be involved in this project; Louise wanted it for herself. She made this clear to her team. However, the senior director in the business wanted Cara and frequently asked her to attend meetings, knowing full well that Louise did not approve. He sometimes called Cara into his office, with no notice or explanation, 'for a chat', but it turned out to be a project meeting of all the key stakeholders. Cara would then be torn – should she tell Louise what had happened? When she did, she was reprimanded by Louise. She was told not to answer his e-mails, not to take calls from him and certainly not to attend meetings. The problem was that this had a negative impact, not just on the development programme, but also on how Cara – and the rest of HR – was perceived in the business. Ultimately, Cara left the business, because she did not know how to solve this problem, which did not relate just to this project but to a whole host more.

Another circumstance in which it is almost inevitable that you will receive conflicting instructions is when you operate within a matrix structure. This is when you essentially have two bosses.

For instance, one might be responsible for a region while the other covers a product line. And you report to both. People who work within a matrix structure often report being pulled in two directions. They complain that each boss thinks their work is more important and should be given priority.

So what do you do if you find yourself caught in the middle? The first thing to consider is whether it actually matters. Since it is such a common issue, many people feel torn at times. Is it possible to accommodate the situation? Do you want to? This is only acceptable if you're not going to be hurt in the process. You want to be a facilitator – make things happen – rather than a whipping boy. Determine what the business requires: who is actually right? Think about the balance of power and who has a hold over you. Then you can decide what kind of balance to strike in meeting the differing needs.

Make sure that the way in which your performance is measured is clear to all. In most organizations, people are set objectives. However, quite frequently, these objectives have little relevance to what the individual actually does. You have to make sure that your own goals and targets are clear and reflective of your contribution. When you are asked to get involved in a piece of work, make sure your objectives are changed to reflect this. Talk to all the parties involved – even if it's a brief conversation – and agree with them what your involvement should be. If a contradiction emerges, you can then document this and talk to your boss(es) to clarify the situation.

However, the setting of objectives is unlikely to be enough, particularly when it's less a question of a particular project and more about general disagreements and day-to-day operating. If you find yourself in this situation, you will need to determine, quite clearly, whether you are on one side or neither. Decide what is appropriate in the circumstances. Is it possible for you to take a balanced approach? Once you have established this, you will need to air the issue with both parties. Try face to face first and see if you can gain agreement. But if the problem persists, you might need – very carefully and sensitively – to put your understanding in writing. In some circumstances, it's possible to copy both parties and ask for their steer in terms of how you should proceed. This would not have been possible in the case study above. Quite the reverse: it would have inflamed the situation. Instead, Cara, by her own admission, felt the answer lay in tackling her boss. Chapter 6 in this book, on 'Mastering the art of influence and persuasion', Chapter 7 on 'Understanding and handling conflict' and Chapter 9 on 'Managing your boss' contain some useful, general advice that could have helped Cara.

Someone stealing your credit

There are many ways in which another person can steal the credit for your work. They might put their own name on a report that you have produced. Or underestimate your input – sometimes to the point of denying you've had any involvement at all. Or pass your ideas off as their own. Or even, in extreme circumstances, *quite literally* steal your work. We recently encountered a manager who had gained access to team members' e-mails. He not only monitored personal e-mail traffic but also copied some of the files and started to work on the ideas in parallel.

It's a widespread problem: almost half the people who responded to our most recent survey said they'd experienced someone else taking the credit for something they had done over the last 12 months. Interestingly, those in the Star or Naive camps were far more likely to have experienced this than Barbarians or Machiavellians.

CASE STUDY

Andrea worked for a law firm. She had spent many years cultivating a relationship with a potential client, although no fees had yet been generated. Andrea had made presentations to the company's legal department, sent pertinent information through, kept up to date on developments in the sector and regularly met the head of legal for coffee. Finally, Andrea's hard work paid off and her firm was successful in becoming one of the 'panel' of law firms representing the company. A partner in another department had participated in the final presentation and he took all the credit for the new business win. Not only did Andrea receive no recognition for her contribution, but at her next appraisal she received a poor rating on her contribution to generating new business, which caused her to drop down a category in her overall rating for the year.

It is important to recognize that it doesn't always matter if someone is credited with your work. Some savvy people do this deliberately. It's part of their influencing technique: to sow the seed of an idea and work in the background to get others to accept their suggestions, without realizing whose they are. They see it as a sign of their success. Alternatively, the practice might be institutionalized; in many organizations, the culture dictates that an individual's main function in life is to make their manager look good. It is accepted that the team will do most of the legwork but the finished product will bear the boss's name. But what can you do when there is no justification for credit being stolen?

On occasion, the practice is blatant – someone quite clearly has taken the credit for something you have done. No attempt has been made to disguise the fact. In these situations it's usually wise to confront the issue, to avoid it happening in the future.

Talk to the person. Try to keep the conversation objective and rational. Point out what has happened rather than criticize them personally. In some circumstances, it might also be helpful to adopt a 'faux naïf' manner: 'I was quite surprised when this happened. Perhaps I've misunderstood?' You might want to appeal to their sense of decency and fair play. But your objective must be to try to ensure that the other person is left in no doubt as to your view of their behaviour, and to seek their assurances that it won't happen again. Use your problem-solving skills to discuss with them how you can work together in the future.

More difficult, however, is when the behaviour is not overt, but more subtle, and you can't be sure that their action is a deliberate move. On such occasions, it would be unwise to confront the other person assertively; instead, you may want to have a conversation just exploring the situation. Some people find that this behaviour continues for months, or even years, and they're never quite sure if it's a blatant act on the part of the other person. They then need to use a range of tactics to deal with the issue. An increase in general communication can help. By copying interested parties in on the work you're involved with, on a regular basis, it becomes more difficult for someone else to claim they've done all the work. But don't do this in an aggressive way. Instead, position the information as helpful: 'Given our conversation yesterday, I thought that it might be useful for you to see what our team has been up to.' Copy other people in on the message, but try to ensure that they at least have some interest! You might want to go further and suggest that you formalize the arrangement and collaborate on that aspect of the work.

In a similar way to the situation described above, where you're caught in the middle, ensuring that objectives and expectations are clear can really help. You need to spell out what you're responsible for and make sure that other people know about this. If someone else wants to contribute towards you achieving your goals, then let them! But make sure that you don't fall into the same trap; if they help, give them the credit for it.

Determine who is responsible for judging your performance and make sure that they understand your contribution. If need be, talk to them about the other individual(s) who might be claiming the credit for your work. Seek their advice about how to deal with the situation. Nine times out of ten, they will probably tell you not to worry about it – but will have logged the problem, which is the important thing.

Someone encroaching on your territory

A linked, but distinct, issue relates to someone encroaching on your territory. Why is this different? Because it is when another person doesn't only claim your credit but they also want your job or at least a part of it. They might be after:

- your roles and responsibilities;
- your job title;
- your project(s);
- your intellectual property;
- your client or supplier relationships;
- your internal network;
- your leadership role.

Why does it happen? Apart from the obvious – you've got a great role and someone else would like it – there is a variety of other reasons. When promoted, many people refuse to rise to their new responsibilities. They continue to get involved in all their old areas of work, essentially doing the job of the person below them. The opposite can also be true: someone who's snapping at their boss's heels, keen to move into their shoes. Or, of course, the attack might be lateral – from rival teams, close colleagues and even external contacts or competitors. It's basically anyone with sharp elbows, keen to have a piece of your action. And the effect? You have your authority under-mined (something 44 per cent of people say they've experienced in the last year).

CASE STUDY

Karl worked as a relationship manager. He and his colleagues were each responsible for a group of clients, generally organized according to territory, one of Karl's key areas being Turkey. On one occasion, he went to visit a Turkish client and was told that his colleague, Marika, had been in to meet with them the previous week. Although the client was reasonably understanding about the confusion, it was quite embarrassing for Karl. He tried to talk to Marika on a number of occasions about what had happened, but she seemed to be avoiding him. Before he'd had the chance to confront her, it happened again with another client. Karl was furious and insisted that Marika discuss the matter with him as soon as he was back in the office again. Marika told him that she had the authorization from a very senior manager in the business to approach 'key target clients', in whichever jurisdictions she wanted, as part of a business development initiative. It turned out that Marika had proposed this initiative to the senior manager some months earlier and he had accepted. Karl was only one of a number of relationship managers who were affected; it seemed that Marika had been given carte blanche to see which clients she pleased – with the boss's blessing.

If this happens to you, your first action has to be to point out to the culprit what they're doing. You never know, it might be a misunderstanding. Assume the best and avoid paranoia – at least at the outset! But when it seems that the problem is not going to go away merely by talking, you will need a strategy for dealing with it. It goes without saying that, in these circumstances, most people want to protect their turf, so let's assume that this is your objective.

It will help you if the scope of your role is clearly documented. Job descriptions and job profiles outline your responsibilities in a clear and unambiguous fashion. Paradoxically, they have become even more important in these rapidly changing times, when people feel they've got no time to do it and can't see the point anyway, since 'it'll probably change again soon!' You need to insist on clarity and make sure that your manager agrees in writing that this is your role.

Then think about other people who have an interest, especially those who are influential. How can you bring them on side? Think laterally. What are the advantages to these people of you remaining and performing well in your current role? The more people you can link your responsibilities with, and the more people who will benefit from your doing it well, the less successful the encroacher is likely to be. Avoid whining and pleading at all costs; instead, be constructive and interesting.

Once you have marshalled your champions, you then need to consider how you will get the other person to back off. This will depend on the type of character you're dealing with. It's easier with a Barbarian than it is with a Machiavellian, because they're likely to have less support. But since both are highly self-motivated and self-interested, the most effective tactic will be to convince them that something else will be better for them personally. You might be able to divert their attention, not by pointing them at another victim, but by helping them to see greater opportunities in their current role. Think about how they're motivated – what *is* it about that aspect of your job that makes them so desperate to take it on – what's in it for them? Then see if this need can be satisfied in a different way. Alternatively, it might be possible to flag up to them all the disadvantages of what they're after. Don't do it in an obvious way, because they are unlikely to believe you. And certainly don't lie. But if you can somehow convey that the work is not lucrative, glamorous, high profile, rewarding – or whatever it is they're after – then you might just put them off.

These are all indirect strategies. As an alternative, or even as a follow-up tactic, you may need to be more direct and confront them. If you have already tried this, you must think about how this conversation is going to be different. Clearly, it will help if you have evidence and allies. So prepare all the relevant facts. Think about the tack you need to take. What is your objective? What is the personality of the other individual? What approaches might work? What will you go to the wire for? And what won't you? You might want to call their bluff and try out a few 'what if' scenarios: 'OK, so I could hand this over in its entirety to you – even though stakeholders A, B and C are not keen – but if I did this, how would it work?' Some people find that this type of discussion does, in fact, generate ideas for collaborative working between the two individuals and their teams. Be assertive and keep your desired outcome in mind at all times. If you've done your homework and secured your support, there is a high chance that they will come around to your way of thinking. But if a stalemate situation develops, try to ensure that you at least agree what the next step is; the situation should not be allowed to fester for too long.

You might then need help, ideally from your manager, but perhaps from HR or a mentor elsewhere in the business. Remember that some of these cases end in claims for constructive dismissal, so it's in the business's interest for the people in power to help you out. Overall, protecting your turf involves clarification, exploration, documentation – and the support of powerful stakeholders – always with your desired outcome firmly in mind.

Being the victim of a smear campaign

Most people have experienced other people talking negatively about them behind their backs. In fact, 40 per cent of people say that this has happened to them in the last year – interestingly, more men than women! If it's happened to you, you will know how upsetting it can be, even on a one-off basis. But when it's constant, relentless – and evident that someone clearly has it in for you – it can be soul destroying.

CASE STUDY

The number two in a global organization found himself the victim of what was described as a 'boardroom ambush'. Sources say that his boss – the general manager – felt threatened by his number two and sought to discredit him. He made up allegations of drunken and lecherous behaviour at a company party. Despite being cleared by an internal investigation, the number two was fired. He sought redress in the courts, but, at the time of writing, the case was ongoing.

It's easy to be overwhelmed by your feelings when it comes to light that someone else has been spreading rumours about you, but objectivity is required. You need to stand back and assess matters, almost separating yourself from the wrongdoing. Focus first on the substance of the allegation. On the basis that 'there's no smoke without fire', could there be some truth in the matter? If there is, this may not excuse the other person's behaviour, but it does guide you in terms of your strategy for dealing with the situation.

Ultimately, the aim will be to clear your name. But what will that require? If the accusations are utterly untrue, then you need to deny them and make sure that others believe you. If the matter is more subjective – and, if you look at things from a slightly different perspective, you can see where they're coming from – then you may need to correct perceptions. However, if the criticisms are true, you must first change your behaviour and then rebuild your reputation.

Think about what, when and who:

What: Given the smear campaign is in full flow, what is your reputation now? How do others perceive you? What are you supposed to have done? Compare this to how you would *like* to be perceived. What is the gap? How can you best go about bridging this gap?

When: Try to identify how long the rumours have been circulating. Clearly, it is far better if you've caught the problem early, but some people find that slurs have been spreading for months, if not years. It's just that no one saw fit to tell them. In these circumstances, it might be harder to shift perceptions, since the negative view may well have become the 'received wisdom'.

Who: Although it's difficult to establish, you will need to know how wide reaching the smear campaign has become. Who knows? Who told them? Is it just a handful of people in one team? Or has the grapevine been so efficient that everyone knows?

You will inevitably need to talk to the individual responsible at some point. Your approach will differ according to whether you're adopting a 'deny', 'adjust' or 'change' strategy. Clearly, you must let them know that you consider their behaviour to be unacceptable. But, given the 'no smoke without fire' argument, you may also want to understand where they're coming from. If you can acknowledge and even agree on a few minor points, they are more likely to shift their perception of you. However, don't accede for the sake of it; make sure that you do, indeed, get their drift. Remember too that it's possible to empathize with the person without necessarily agreeing with what they're saying: 'I can see that would have been difficult for you.' In some instances, it is good to build bridges – even if it's just to avoid the same thing happening again. In any case, you should aim to agree the way forward, which might include them 'issuing' some form of apology and helping you as you try to rebuild your reputation.

And this is the key part of the whole thing: people's opinions of you have to change. You might get others to help you – your manager, for instance – but, generally speaking, you'll need to be spearheading the efforts yourself. In some circumstances, it's possible just to correct the perception – put the record straight. This is a tactic that works best when the allegations are patently unfounded, untrue. You can talk to the people who have been 'infected' and demonstrate that the rumours are falsehoods. Or you may even be able to provide documentary evidence that contradicts the gossip. So, for instance, an individual who dis-covered that he had been widely criticized for underperforming across a range of measures was able to demonstrate that he had, in fact, achieved all his objectives.

However, when the issue is more subjective – a matter of opinion – you might need to use other, more subtle, ways of correcting people's perceptions. Go back to your gap analysis. What is your reputation now, compared with how you would like it to be? What therefore can you do in order to shift others' views? Clearly, actions speak louder than words. But don't only do it, let people *know* that you're doing it too: communication is critical. This might feel uncomfortable to some, but it's absolutely necessary. There may also be scope to talk to selected people about what's happened and why you think it's wrong, and then get their views. Share with them what you plan to do to address the situation. Seek their input. Ask them what you need to do to get things back on track. But choose them wisely and let them know that you're not discussing the matter with all and sundry. If you've selected the right people, they will become advocates for you, quashing any residual rumours. For further help, you might want to read Chapter 12, 'Making the right impression'.

And finally, make sure that any measurement of your performance reflects the true situation; you don't want to be penalized at appraisal time.

Dealing with hidden agendas

The majority of people at work will be alert to hidden agendas, but many are content to guess at what's going on. They stick with their assumptions, which may or may not be correct. They fail to uncover the real intent or discontent of the other party. Savvy people, however, are perceptive about others and interested in their views. They are concerned if their colleagues appear to be unhappy. And if someone appears to be acting in an underhand way, they want to know why. They uncover – and deal with – hidden agendas.

CASE STUDY

A senior person, Michael, applied for, but failed to get, the top
job. This went to an outsider, Andrew, who also happened to be
a specialist in the same area as Michael. Michael accepted the
decision and prepared to carry on as before, determined to serve
his new boss as best he could. There was a long delay before the
new person arrived, during which Michael was surprised to have
no contact from Andrew. When Andrew did arrive, he showed
absolutely no interest in being briefed by Michael, and wasted
no time saying that he disapproved not only of Michael's
management style but also of his whole approach to the job.
An error occurred in one of the areas that Michael was responsible
for and he was astonished to find himself facing disciplinary
proceedings along with the direct report whose area it was.
Andrew publically berated both Michael and his direct report.
When Michael went to see Andrew to remonstrate, he was told
that Andrew considered this to be a resignation issue: he was
expecting Michael to leave the organization. The agenda behind
the decision to take disciplinary proceedings against a very senior
colleague – which had never happened in this organization before
– was in fact the first step in a campaign to get rid of Michael who
had, one month earlier, received a national award for outstanding
contribution to the field – the first person in the organization ever
to be honoured in this way. We can but guess at what lay behind
Andrew's hidden agenda. Did he feel threatened by Michael? Was
he jealous of Michael's award? Whatever his motives, Andrew's
behaviour was widely perceived to be barbaric.

A small minority are happily oblivious to hidden agendas. They
take things at face value and believe what people tell them.
'Are you happy with this?' they ask. 'Absolutely,' says the other
person, whilst clearly betraying they're not – with their tone of
voice and their body language. These people frequently fall into

the Naive camp. If this is you, it is vital that you watch for the signals and notice when people are dissatisfied, hiding something, being evasive or paying lip service. Think about what people actually do compared with what they say they'll do. Watch others; how do they react to the individual in question?

But once you've spotted a hidden agenda item, what do you do about it? If there's time, you could talk to other people. Have they noticed? What do they think it's all about? Be careful about how you position your question. Asking if they think X is all right is very different from giving your observation – especially if you haven't spoken to X first. If you do this, you are behaving every bit as badly as X, if not worse, by talking about them behind their back. Think about factors which could be influencing the way they're acting. Have there been developments in the business which might affect them – either positively or negatively? Could they be angling for a particular opportunity? Have the dynamics of the team changed? And so on.

These are all, of course, assumptions and it makes sense to check them out. You could talk to the person one to one, treading carefully, of course, and making sure you position the conversation constructively. The chances are, however, that they will tell you everything's fine, that you're imagining it. This is when many people shrug their shoulders and walk away. However, if it's clear to all that they have a hidden agenda, it's best to give them the feedback. Try not to come across as though you don't believe them, but you can talk about the impression they're conveying and the impact it's having. Some hidden agendas are subconscious: the individual in question has no idea that that is what's driving them. Having the conversation can help to raise awareness – even if the admission takes a while to emerge.

This might still be unsuccessful, but at least you've tried. What happens then? Well, you need to keep a watching brief. Observe what happens. Of course, it might not matter in the slightest if the other person has a hidden agenda. That could be their own business. But if it has an adverse effect on someone – and that includes themselves – then it makes sense to keep an eye on things. Above all, try to avoid being caught unawares or caught in crossfire.

Being held down

The last big issue of the six relates to career development. It's your life and your career – and you have aspirations – and so to feel that someone else is limiting those can cause immense personal stress and demoralization. It can also lead to a loss of confidence – and perhaps even competence.

CASE STUDY

During our research, we encountered four separate people to whom the same thing had happened. Their organizations had each launched flexible working for senior staff, usually amid much publicity and fanfare. And our four individuals had all adopted the flexible arrangements. Their colleagues were intolerant; they complained when any one of them left 'early', or worked from home. This started to be reflected in their feedback and appraisals. Despite the fact that each person was achieving agreed objectives, they were perceived not to be performing. They were also told – two overtly, but two more subtly – that they would never be promoted whilst they continued to work flexibly.

When it comes to career development, there is a difference between women and men. Men are more likely to ask their boss about a move to the next level, and they do it at an earlier stage.

Women will frequently already be operating at that level, but still feel uncomfortable asking for promotion. Everyone recognizes that it is necessary to take ownership of their own career, but there are varying degrees of comfort with outlining aspirations and registering interest. A Machiavellian manager failed to put his female team member forward for promotion because she didn't ask him. He knew that she was ready but, being Middle Eastern, she said it was culturally impossible for her to ask. He admitted to playing games with her.

Assuming you have made your desires clear, however, and you feel as though you're being held down, what do you do? No matter how difficult it might be to have the conversation, you need to talk to your manager about what it would take to move you to the next level. When confronted in this way, many bosses become evasive or vague. That's not good enough, so you will need to utilize your questioning skills to establish clear and measurable targets. Brace yourself, though; the answer might be that you would never be ready for promotion (at least in the eyes of this boss or this organization) and so you'd probably be wise to think about moving on. But it's better to know than to be strung along, not least since your boss's opinion might not be the prevailing view elsewhere in the company. You could then think about moving to another department or team.

Assuming that your manager is positive, and you have set targets for yourself, you then need to think about your stock in the business. Do people know you? What would they say about you? There's no doubt that profile and reputation play an important role when it comes to identifying those who are ready for promotion. You may need to volunteer for projects and find (sound, plausible) reasons for meeting key stakeholders in the business.

If, by contrast, your manager hasn't played ball and you actually want to stay, you will have an uphill struggle on your hands. But all is not lost. You could talk to HR. If your manager is discriminating against you, there are clear policies and procedures that you will need to follow and HR will be able to advise you what these are.

In extreme circumstances, you might want to talk to your boss's boss, but be aware that this is the 'nuclear option' when it comes to boss relations. For further assistance, Chapter 9, 'Managing your boss', contains some useful information. And if you feel that it's a matter of profile, Chapter 12, 'Making the right impression', might help.

As mentioned at the beginning of this chapter, there are probably as many challenging political situations as there are days of the year. We are exploring just six – which, according to our research, are those most widely experienced – but no doubt you will have others. Reading through the remainder of this book will furnish you with a toolkit which, once mastered, will enable you to deal with most of the flak you are likely to encounter at work: in short, the savvy to survive in organizational life.

Chapter Six
Mastering the art of influence and persuasion

An HR manager in a City law firm, when asked 'What is political savvy?' replied as follows:

To me it means being aware who one needs to have on side to get certain decisions made, who are the important parties in progressing a project, who you might need to get on board, and also who can help you to push forward your agenda. It can also mean being aware of who to not annoy or upset, or exclude from something.

Influence and persuasion are fundamental components of savvy. It's all very well knowing what's coming down the line and being massively insightful, but if you can't get others to do what you want them to do, then you can't be described as savvy! In Chapter 2, we emphasized the importance of taking a positive, proactive approach. This is critical: you're unlikely to have an impact on events and achieve your aims unless you are prepared to take action. But this is not enough; there are those people around us who, with the best will in the world, seem completely unable to exert their influence. Or worse still, they manage to provoke precisely the opposite reaction. These people are ineffective influencers – irrespective of how good their ideas are objectively, other people seem determined to thwart them.

Influence is all about ensuring that things go your way. This might sound Machiavellian, but remember that being savvy involves not just being effective but doing it for honourable reasons. So, assuming that this is the case, the next question is: how can you get other people to say 'yes' to you? Ideally, of course, they should comply because they *want* to – they see the sense, they are excited by the prospect, they believe it's the right way to go, or they just think so highly of you that they'd do whatever you asked them. Less ideal is the situation where people conform to your requests but are unhappy about it. Though in the real world this may be the best you can hope for. It could be an unpleasant job, for instance, or a regulatory requirement, or a task that sits firmly outside the other individual's comfort zone. There are all sorts of reasons why someone might be reluctant to go the way you want them to go. The trick is to recognize this and have at your disposal a full portfolio of influencing techniques, so that you can not only sway their thinking but also minimize the potential downside.

Step 1: determine who to influence

Sometimes it's patently clear who you need to influence. On other occasions, it's not so obvious. And there may be a number of different people – fulfilling different roles – who you need to take into consideration. These include:

- decision makers;
- gatekeepers;
- known opponents;
- known advocates;
- opinion formers;
- end users.

When you think about exerting your influence, the *decision maker* is often the first person who springs to mind – and, in a simple scenario, could be the only individual you need to talk to. But when it's a more complicated situation, with a large number of interested parties, the decision maker might be the *last* person you want to approach. Find out what constraints they could be under, what other factors might be in play and whether the decision maker has any 'previous form' in this kind of situation.

Establish too who is likely to be advising them, whose counsel they tend to heed. Some of these people might be *gatekeepers*. Most commonly, gatekeepers are considered to be the people who grant or deny you access – such as a secretary or PA. You certainly need to develop a relationship with them. But more importantly – and perhaps less obviously – you have the people who ultimately make recommendations, and whose advice the decision maker will seek out and respect. Without considering these individuals, you could invest a huge amount of time working on the decision maker only to find that a failure to persuade the gatekeeper means that it's a flat 'no'.

And then you have the *opponents* and the *advocates*. It's often tempting to ignore or to try to circumnavigate your enemies, just hoping that they'll go away. But it's far more useful to understand where their resistance stems from, since this will help you to build your case and increase your chances of bringing them around to your way of thinking. Without this knowledge, you have little chance of doing so. Besides, the 'conversion' of an adversary or someone who's known to be highly cynical is usually a powerful endorsement of your argument.

Bizarrely, many people pay too little attention to their allies/ advocates – focusing, instead, on those who are likely to get in the way. This is a mistake – and a missed opportunity to add weight to your proposal, provide evidence to support it and create a groundswell of support. The advocate may well be able to help you with tactical advice.

Opinion formers are the unofficial thought leaders. They might be in this position because everyone likes them and respects their views. Alternatively – or additionally – they could be specialists or experts in the field. This would, of course, include external advisors.

Finally, it might make sense to involve some *end users* – the people who will ultimately be most affected by the decision.

Clearly, not all these roles will be fulfilled in all influencing scenarios. And when they are, it may be necessary, for practical reasons, to segment your audience, grouping together the people who play the different roles and considering whether one influencing strategy will work for each of the segments.

Step 2: establish your influencing strategy

Surprisingly, a large number of people have no influencing strategy. Instead, they just wade in – and seem surprised when things don't turn out the way they wanted. Savvy people appreciate the importance of spending time considering what result they want and how they're most likely to get it. The diagram in Figure 6.1 illustrates a simple influencing strategy.

Of critical importance is your desired outcome. This may sound obvious, but on occasion we either fool ourselves or we're not 100 per cent sure what the best result would be. Take, for instance, the senior banker who had a real problem with a trader who was rude, inconsiderate and prone to angry outbursts, even in front of important stakeholders. Initially, the manager stated

FIGURE 6.1

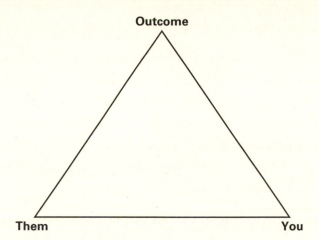

that he wanted to influence the trader to change his behaviour. However, on examination, he had to admit that this would not have been a good outcome. The trader was actually in the wrong job. So, instead, the manager really wanted to persuade him to move into another role – one which was more suited to his strengths and in which his bad behaviour would affect only himself.

So be clear and honest with yourself about your desired outcome. Make sure that you establish exactly what you want to achieve before entering into the debate. And be open to the possibility that you may have more than one objective: yes, you do want to 'win', but an important part of your outcome might revolve around how you want the other person to feel, once you've brought them round to your point of view.

Then turn your attention to what is likely to influence the other person. What do you think their desired outcome is? Perhaps more importantly, how well do you understand their personality? Are they highly rational or more intuitive? Do they like time to think before responding or do they prefer to chat things through? Are they detailed or more big picture? All of these aspects should have an impact on how you choose to position your arguments with them, when and how you approach them and what supporting information you might need.

Which brings us to the third component of your influencing strategy – you! As a consequence of what you've gleaned so far, how will you go about influencing others? What do you have to prepare? What behaviours do you need to adopt? Should you get others on side with your arguments? What levers can you pull? What kind of language will you use? And what can you offer them in return?

You need to have thought all of this through – even if it's just for a few minutes – before you approach the other individual. But be careful not to become too attached to your game plan: sometimes the mere fact that you have prepared yourself makes it more difficult for you to show sufficient flexibility. Being responsive to what's said is a vital aspect of influencing and it might be necessary to modify your approach – or even revise your ideal outcome – once you become engaged with the other person. The fact is that many people who are most effective at influencing believe that having a clear strategy and accepting its limitations are what enable them to deviate from the strategy, since they're confident they know what impact any deviation will have. In short, focus on your strategy but be flexible about tactics.

Step 3: follow some basic rules

The type of influencing style you use must be appropriate for the specific situation and the different audiences you are dealing with. More about this later! There are, however, some *general* principles that apply when you are planning to influence another person:

- Put yourself into the shoes of the recipient – what would be a good outcome for them, what are they thinking and feeling? The more you understand their motivations and concerns, the more in tune with them you become and the more likely you are to be able to influence them.

- Concentrate on the recipient – make eye contact, be genuinely interested in them and try to form an alliance with them.

- Mirror and match them – when rapport exists naturally, you will notice that two people sit in a similar way, use common language and demonstrate the same energy levels. When this rapport is not there initially, you need to create it. Mirroring and matching the body language of the other person is a good way to generate chemistry.

- Then lead – once you are 'in rapport' with the other person, you can start to lead them. For instance, if your proposals were initially met with apathy, you might first mirror the energy levels, in an empathetic way, and then slowly manoeuvre the other person around to a more enthusiastic demeanour. Your starting point might be this: 'OK, I can see you're not sold on this yet. What extra information can I give you to help convince you?'

- Demonstrate mutual support – if you talk about 'we', rather than 'I', you are instantly creating the impression that you are in this together. This simple switch in language can also change the emphasis from a debate that is potentially adversarial to one that is focused on problem solving.

- Look for common ground – for many of us our first reaction is to focus on areas of difference. It's almost human nature to do so. Instead, where possible, seek areas of agreement – congruence – and seek to exploit them.

- Concentrate on your non-verbal signals – gestures, posture and tone of voice send far more information to the other person than the words you are using. It is therefore important to make sure that your non-verbal behaviours all add up to 'I am trustworthy and I really want us to make this work.' And of course, it's easier to achieve this outcome if you are operating on their level rather than acting apart. So try to:

- go through in advance what you want to achieve and why;
- feel comfortable about what you are asking for;
- be open and honest, while remaining sensitive to the other person's needs, wants and feelings;
- be truly committed to a win–win situation.

- Don't press on when you have achieved your outcome. Many people continue to 'influence' once the other person has already agreed to their demands, which is not only annoying but might also make the other party change their mind again!

- Listen. This last point is so fundamental to being an effective influencer that it merits a section of its own …

Step 4: listen

So often, when we're thinking about influencing another person, we focus almost all our attention on what we're going to say, forgetting one of the most critical aspects of influence: listening. A director of a large retail organization expressed surprise that this important skill is considered to be a part of the overall influence and persuasion toolkit. 'But surely,' he said, 'you're not going to be able to persuade anyone of anything if you're just sitting there saying nothing.' He wasn't convinced until a colleague used the analogy of a salesperson: 'Who would you prefer to buy from – the person who bores you rigid for hours about product features and superior quality, or the one who listens carefully to your issues, seems to understand them, and then pipes up at the last minute with a solution to your problems?' He was then convinced.

But listening is quite difficult to do properly. You need terrific powers of concentration and tenacity to listen 100 per cent of the time. There are also different levels:

- *Level one – listening superficially*: This is where you merely pick up the thread of what a person is saying. You may be able to repeat the last five words they've used, but you haven't *really* heard them. This type of conversation tends to be very one way and the individual doing the talking might lose confidence and interest in what they themselves are saying.

- *Level two – listening for information*: Here you pick up all the facts and figures and are listening on the surface, but you are unaware of the feelings and emotions which accompany what the individual is saying. The conversation will be more two way than at Level one, but the type of question asked will be all about what happened, when did it happen – questions designed to elicit hard data. In this situation, you can find yourself ignoring pleas for help and fixing symptoms rather than causes.

- *Level three – listening for feelings and emotions*: Here you are much more aware of what is going on behind the words. You are watching for the non-verbal signals and probing far more in your questioning. The type of question asked will be about *why* things happened or *why* they feel that way. This enables you to get to the heart of the problem. It also makes the other individual feel important and valued as a person – a very persuasive mix.

If you want to influence others more successfully, it is vital for you to listen at Level three. But avoid making assumptions. Carefully crafted, open questions will ensure that you can get to the heart of matters and pick up on what's most important to the other person without getting the wrong end of the stick. Other tips for active listening are:

- Stop talking – especially that internal, mental silent chatter – and answering back. Try to withhold comment and let the other person finish. Often the core of an issue – or argument or idea – can be in the last few words. This is particularly important when we are in a thoroughly familiar situation. We tend to finish someone's sentence for them ourselves and work out a reply instead of listening to what they are actually saying.

- Care – you must care enough about the other person and their point of view to listen actively to them. You must also want to improve your listening skills. Without this motivation, it's too much effort.

- Relax – research shows that tension reduces the effectiveness of our auditory receptors. So a good listener must be relaxed.

- Find an uninterrupted area if possible and keep away from distractions, as they will spoil the flow.

- Be aware of your personal prejudices and make a conscious effort to stop them influencing your judgement.

- Pay attention – put the speaker at ease by demonstrating that you are listening. The good listener doesn't look over someone's shoulder, or text while they are talking. Show you're listening by nodding, maintaining eye contact and exhibiting engaged body language. We rely on the expression on another person's face to tell us how we are faring in a conversation.

- Try not to rush the discussion. Give time to the person.

- If you do have to take notes, explain what you are doing and check it's OK. Blame your poor memory. Make it clear that your note taking is a tribute to the interest or importance of what you are hearing. And look at the person – not at your paper!

- Check back – try to restate what the other person has just said, using their words as far as possible. They can then feel confident that what you heard is what they wanted to say. It also helps *you* to reflect.

- Build – develop the other person's argument or position, but avoid using it as a technique to knock down their ideas and substitute yours.

- Be supportive – express your interest and encourage the speaker to continue.

- Structure – help the speaker to develop and structure their idea. Summarize and agree the main points before moving on.

- Be alert to what the speaker is *not* saying as well as what they are saying. Very often what is missing is more important than what is there.

- Pay attention to non-verbal signals such as body language.

Step 5: use the right influencing tactics

So far, we've covered the key people you need to influence, your strategy for doing so, some basic rules and the art of active listening. If you haven't followed these guidelines in the past and you start to do so now, your influence will increase. However, to take it to the next level, it is vital to choose the right influencing tactics. Different people like different things. What will appeal to one individual – and encourage them to commit to you – may be a turn-off for another. Furthermore, different circumstances require different approaches. Highly influential people have the ability to evaluate the person and the situation, and then apply an appropriate style. In order to be successful, the tactic you choose should be:

- ethical and socially acceptable;
- used for a legitimate request;
- appropriate, given your status and relationship with the person you are trying to influence;
- skilfully used;
- consistent with the individual's values;
- appropriate for the individual's personality.

Broadly speaking, influencing tactics fall into two different categories: *push* techniques, which actively steer an individual towards a particular course of action; and *pull* techniques, which are far more subtle and tend to draw the individual in. While there is some overlap between the two, push actions are more akin to persuasion, and pull techniques are associated with influence.

Where would you say you fall? Think about the influencing techniques that you use from day to day. Then answer the questions in Table 6.2, awarding yourself the appropriate score (see Table 6.1) according to whether you use this type of technique.

TABLE 6.1

• Never	score 1 point
• Occasionally	score 2 points
• An average amount	score 3 points
• Fairly frequently	score 4 points
• Very frequently	score 5 points

TABLE 6.2

	Score		Score		Score		Score
1. I appeal to others' values and aspirations.		2. I am careful to listen to others.		3. I am always ready with the facts and figures to back my argument.		4. I'm not averse to exchanging favours in order to get things done.	
5. I excite others by the way I speak.		6. I readily admit to things I have done wrong.		7. I can quickly see flaws in others' ideas.		8. I make it clear to people what I expect from them.	
9. I focus on team achievement.		10. I seek others' suggestions before offering my own ideas.		11. I can be relied on to come up with a new idea.		12. I reward people for their success.	
13. I appeal to common goals and objectives.		14. I am open about my own personal concerns.		15. I am prepared to enlist others to back my argument.		16. I'm not afraid to deal with poor performance.	

TABLE 6.2 *continued*

	Score		Score		Score		Score
17. I can put into words things that other people only dream about.		18. I give people responsibility for important tasks.		19. I will use my position/status to get my proposals agreed.		20. I apply pressure where necessary, to get what I want done.	
21. I generate a feeling of 'We're in this together.'		22. I really try to put myself into the shoes of others.		23. I love the cut and thrust of a good logical debate.		24. I like to bargain and negotiate with people.	
25. I am confident that we can achieve.		26. I always make sure that I have understood properly.		27. I am usually ready with a counter argument.		28. I believe that most people are motivated by fear or greed.	
29. I am able to paint a very vivid, and exciting, picture.		30. I make sure that everyone has a chance to voice their opinion.		31. I am happy to defend my ideas.		32. I always praise people for a job well done.	
Column 1 total		**Column 2 total**		**Column 3 total**		**Column 4 total**	

The higher you score in any one column, the more likely you are to use a particular influencing technique (described below). A score of 28 or more in any one column is a high score. However, this is not just about high or low scores – one person could award themselves all 5s, while someone else, who behaves in a similar way, awards 3s and 4s. Instead, it is about the appropriateness of the techniques you are using: 'Is what I'm doing right, given the circumstances and the individual concerned?' Study the four paragraphs below, which describe the techniques used in each column.

> Column 1: *charisma – inspirational*. Use of charisma – an inspirational influencing style – is a pull technique. It is all about painting a vivid picture, articulating it in a compelling way and generating a sense of excitement in others. People will then want to be included within your plans and a part of your team. It's also about focusing people on what needs to be done by appealing to their values and aspirations. It is highly appropriate for people who are in a team leadership role or who have to bring others around to their way of thinking, without line management authority. On the whole, people who are described as inspirational and motivational will be adept at using this particular influencing style.

> Column 2: *empathy – personal*. Use of empathy – a highly personal influencing tool – is also a pull technique. Being influenced in this way tends to make people feel valued and valuable, because they have been listened to, their ideas have been understood and the other person has opened up to them. It creates loyalty and trust in a team, and a spirit of selflessness and sacrifice. This influencing technique can be used in all directions – with your boss, your team and your peers – and it increases commitment

to tasks. Bear in mind, however, that it is more likely to appeal to people who are driven by emotion rather than logic, where you may need to supplement your appeal with a few facts and figures.

Column 3: logic – rational. Adopting a logical approach is a push technique. It involves doing your homework, having all the facts and figures at your fingertips, and being prepared to argue your corner – no matter how heated the debate becomes. This is a rational rather than an emotional style of influence. It is appropriate in situations where it is important to have a watertight case, for instance where you are asking management to invest in a project. In this situation, it's vital to assess the costs, articulate the benefits and be able to back your argument cogently. One potential downside associated with this approach is that the recipient knows they are being persuaded and can feel resentful. Used appropriately, however, the logical technique can be applied in any direction, but is *particularly* effective with your boss or with colleagues in other departments over whom you have no direct authority. Why? Because the arguments are often so compelling that the risks seem minimized, the rewards tangible and the business case clear. It is also useful to bear in mind when you are dealing with very logical and/or risk-averse people – almost irrespective of where they sit in the organization and the subject matter.

Column 4: direction – forceful. Again, this is a push style – the carrot and stick were made for this individual! The forceful approach involves stating clearly what is expected from people, rewarding them for success and, of course, punishing them for failures. Achieving goals is very important and so the individual will not be averse to calling in favours or applying pressure – anything to get the job done. When applied in a forceful *manner*, this technique really only works with people over whom you have direct, usually formal, control: the team you lead, for example, or perhaps suppliers. And being a push style, it can again feel uncomfortable on the receiving end. However, when used persuasively, or even passionately, it can be successful in getting others on board and motivated. Furthermore, a low score in this column could mean that you are not being clear about what constitutes good performance. It might also suggest that you are not giving your team the feedback they need – both good and bad. So before congratulating yourself on not using this form of influence, think about the impact that the omission might have.

In the real world, things rarely organize themselves in the clear-cut manner implied in the preceding paragraphs. As a result, you may well find yourself having to use a blend of techniques to achieve your aims, or alternating between push and pull styles. But the key elements of influencing, in broad terms, are:

- getting inside the head of the individual;
- really listening to what they're saying – and not saying;
- adapting your style to help you to achieve your objectives.

CASE STUDY

Ruth is a consultant. After she had nurtured a client organization for many years, there was a change of CEO. The new CEO, Charles, had his own favourite consultants and he had used them for many years. Ruth knew that, politically, her account was at risk and so she had to be savvy. She established her influencing strategy. Lining up key stakeholders was critical; senior managers needed to be vocally positive about the projects that Ruth and her colleagues had been involved with. So Ruth conducted a review of the work undertaken. She did this free of charge, but it was worth it, because the results were good. She then asked the head of strategy to suggest to the new CEO that he and Ruth should meet up. At the meeting, Ruth had decided that she would first use a pull style: she planned to ask questions about his strategy, listen carefully and respond with helpful insights. But she knew that this stage could not last long; he would be looking for ideas and evidence from a consultant. Ruth therefore moved into a rational approach, using her review findings to provide evidence that projects had been successful. She communicated this information in a friendly but assertive way – and was careful not to dwell too long on the data. Ruth handed over a copy of the short report and moved back into a pull style, first asking further questions and then building on Charles's responses by consolidating his thoughts into a vision. She then talked in terms of next steps. Because she had taken care to mirror his body language and develop rapport, she was successful in influencing the new CEO. The account was safe.

And finally ...

We have talked predominantly about overt and active influence – the things you do consciously to bring someone around to your way of thinking. However, you can't not influence! Your presence, or absence, the way you conduct yourself, the impression you convey, the e-mails you send out or fail to send out – in short, everything you do – has an influence in one way or another. It might not be what you'd intended or wanted. In fact, you might achieve exactly the opposite effect. But it's a factor. What impact do you have? In Chapter 12 we talk about your profile and reputation, but here is a little food for thought about other factors which can have an influence.

A staggering 44 per cent of people observe that their colleagues flirt with one another. Interestingly, people who sit within the Barbarian camp are more likely to agree with this statement than others; presumably, this is part of their influencing toolkit! Building on this, over half believe that, where they work, physical attraction plays a part in career development. The results indicated that this is more likely to be the case if you work for a male boss. It's also a practice which is more prevalent in the private sector than the public sector. Surprisingly, those falling into the Star camp are more likely to agree that physical attraction plays a part in career development than other people. Perhaps this is just a reflection of the way the world really works?

Chapter Seven
Understanding and handling conflict

Only 43 per cent of people agree with the statement 'Where I work, we deal with conflict constructively.' Over a third disagree. Interestingly, there is a gender difference. Women are 80 per cent more likely than men to feel that conflict is *not* handled constructively. And this seems to filter through to others; if you work for a female boss, you are more than twice as likely to feel highly dissatisfied with the way conflict is handled in your team.

Conflict exists. There is probably some form of conflict for you every single day at work – and, indeed, at home. It is surprising, then, that many people deny its existence: 'Oh no! There's no conflict in this team. None at all. We're absolutely harmonious.' If this is true, then you could argue there will be no creativity and no challenge; like politics, conflict can be both positive and negative – but usually negative if it's not handled effectively. The denial that conflict exists may be partially attributed to a misunderstanding about what it actually is. Conflict can be defined as 'any situation in which your wants, needs, views or your agenda differ from that of another person'. Conflict is not the same as confrontation, because this implies that you surface the problem. But you can choose whether or not to confront an issue. There may also be conflict without the other person realizing that it exists. Again, it's down to you to decide whether to raise the issue or not.

So why are we looking at conflict? Why is it of relevance when we are exploring the concept of savvy? Well, our research very clearly indicates that much of the negative politicking is the result of conflict. People competing for limited resource, for instance. Or an argument of some kind. Or roles with built-in conflict. Or teams fighting to be given the credit for a successful piece of work. Or two people who just can't stand one another! In business today, you cannot be savvy without possessing the ability to spot conflict – existing or potential – and then deal with it in the most appropriate way.

CASE STUDY

In a high-profile organization, two people were competing for one assistant director role. It was awarded to Maria, the individual who had been recruited into the company more recently and who had less experience in the field, though who was arguably more 'senior'. The other candidate, Lucia, was very disappointed, but was soon afterwards offered a full directorship in another area, without the role being advertised, instantly making her more senior than Maria. This caused a great deal of acrimony between the two. Shortly afterwards, however, Maria's role was made up to director, with the implication that both then needed to collaborate on the same executive team. Worse still, the nature of their roles was such that they had to work very closely together, but with significant built-in tension: Lucia was responsible for managing the relationships with key partners, whilst Maria was accountable for delivery to those partners. Only two very close colleagues could make it work. The relationship deteriorated rapidly. Their executive colleagues couldn't bear the two individuals being in the same room. And the performance of the organization went downhill. Maria seemed keen to tarnish Lucia's reputation at every opportunity. In return, Lucia made it clear to her people that they should not cooperate with Maria's team. It was the job of the chief executive to sort this out, but – being averse to conflict – he did not do so. People who were initially the victims of the negative political situation were dragged into it and found themselves accused of 'playing the politics', merely for having listened to one side or to the other. And the chief executive was held to account, because he did nothing to address the problem. As a consequence of this failure to confront and deal with the conflict, one individual ultimately left the organization – there seemed to be no alternative – raising a grievance as she did so.

The ability to handle conflict is vitally important. But it's something that many people struggle with. So, in this chapter, we look at what happens when things go wrong and what you can do to deal effectively with conflict.

Understand your own approach to conflict

Some people seem to welcome the opportunity to engineer confrontation, whilst others are utterly averse to even the mildest argument. It appears to be an aspect of personality since most of us have a 'typical' response when problems arise. Where do you sit on this continuum? Are you energized by a good row or do you withdraw at the first sign of a conflict? Cast your mind back to the last time you were angry with someone about the way they behaved, or an occasion on which you were placed in an impossible position, or a situation when someone else didn't agree with you. What were your first thoughts? Did they fall into any – or all – of the following categories?

Type one reaction: Oh no, I can't bear this – I really hope things will sort themselves out!

Type two reaction: I'll probably deal with this next week – now's not a good time.

> *Type three reaction*: I'm going to give that bastard a piece of my mind – now.

> *Type four reaction*: Let's sort this out – what outcome are we trying to achieve?

Type one reactions are an *avoidance strategy*: 'If I close my eyes and pretend nothing's happened, it may just go away.' Or it might be: 'I feel completely sick about this and just can't face up to it.' People adopt an avoidance strategy for all sorts of reasons. They may feel highly anxious about the prospect of a confrontation, or they might fear hurting the other person. Or they may genuinely believe that problems usually sort themselves out. In reality, problems rarely disappear of their own accord: what typically happens is that they fester, people demonstrate increasingly unproductive behaviours and, more often than not, the situation deteriorates further.

Type two reactions indicate a *delaying strategy*: 'I'm quite aware there's an issue, but I don't have the time/nerve/inclination to deal with it now. I'll review the situation again in a week's time and see if it's still a problem. It may well have petered out by then, but if it hasn't, I will try to fix it.' What typically happens in this scenario is that the person repeatedly postpones the confrontation up to the point where it is just too embarrassing to deal with. As a result, type two delaying reactions turn into type one avoidance situations. There are many examples of this when annual appraisals come round. People say how surprised they are about what is being said: 'I really wish someone had mentioned this before'.

Type three reactions constitute an *aggressive strategy*: 'How could they do that? I'll show them. By the time I've finished with them, they won't be doing it again in a hurry.' People who follow this behaviour pattern tend to take things very personally and don't take kindly to not getting their own way. They do not avoid issues and they do not allow problems to fester for a long time. But while they are keen to confront problems, they tend to do it in an antagonistic, zero-sum game ('I win, you lose') way. Very often, this approach rubs people up the wrong way. It is counterproductive, because human beings (unlike most other members of the animal kingdom) are programmed to respond to aggression with counter aggression rather than submission.

Type four reactions involve a *problem-solving strategy*: 'I don't like what's happening here, but I'm sure they had their motives for behaving the way they did – let me explore what's happened, then put the matter right.' This approach acknowledges that people act for a reason and works on the basis that, until you know what these reasons are, it's unlikely that you will be able to put in place any concrete actions for the future. An individual using a problem-solving strategy neither avoids nor delays – nor do they charge in like a bull in a china shop. Theirs is a more cooperative, listening, compromising type of approach, which works well – except with that small, but impossible to ignore, sub-population who have no interest in establishing harmonious relationships. Such people – sometimes labelled sociopaths – think that peaceful coexistence is for wimps, and consider a day wasted unless they have reduced a fellow human being to tears!

Which of the above approaches most closely represents your own? It may be that you react to different situations in different ways. Why? There are all sorts of reasons behind why we act the way we do. Table 7.1 lists a few beliefs which can help define why you might fail to deal with conflict effectively.

Which ones can you hear yourself saying or thinking regularly? Are there others? Think carefully and try to develop a clear picture of how you behave in different situations and with different people, and what pattern you typically fall into.

TABLE 7.1

- I have no right.
- I don't have the status.
- I'm not sure of my ground.
- They intimidate me.
- I don't like them.
- I like them.
- They may stop liking me.
- They may stop respecting me.
- I'll show them who's boss.
- I'll teach them to mess with me.
- I'd better get this over and done with.
- It's no big deal.

- I can't be bothered.
- I don't have the time.
- They don't have the time.
- I don't *really* want to solve the problem.
- I don't like hurting people.
- It's trivial for them (but important for me).
- It's too difficult.
- It's too sensitive.
- I don't have all the facts.
- They won't change.

It is important to understand what motivates you – and to be prepared to challenge aspects of your own motivation. If you are really honest with yourself, you may have to admit that many of your reasons for avoiding or delaying confrontation are actually invalid. You generally do have the right to tackle another human being about issues of mutual concern. If you find it uncomfortable to exercise this right, it's a problem worth addressing. You'll need to start by identifying the causes of this discomfort: is it low self-esteem or perhaps the fear of failure that is holding you back? Maybe you don't really want to solve the problem. You're happier to sit back and moan about it, playing the martyr, or perhaps you just want to give the other person a piece of your mind.

Successful conflict resolution requires two things. The first is a *real* desire to solve the problem. The second is the ability to view the situation objectively – even if it is a very personal issue – and to develop an approach that is focused on resolving the conflict rather than merely making yourself feel better. Being clear about the outcome is critical. And, if you are one of those people who doesn't handle conflict well, or doesn't feel too good about it, then the technique of reframing discussed in Chapter 2 can help enormously.

Understand the source of the conflict

Before deciding how to tackle an issue, you need to understand how the conflict arose in the first place. First of all, how real is it? Can you, hand on heart, say that there is a genuine difference of opinion, or are you just feeling personally slighted? Even if it's the latter, you might still choose to act, but you do need to see it for what it is: a dented ego is not the same as a fundamental disagreement. When you're convinced that the conflict exists, then determine who exactly is responsible. Avoid shooting the messenger. Similarly, spare a thought for others who just get caught in the crossfire: the wrong place at the wrong time. It's important to be clear about who it is you are in conflict with. Then try to work out why your protagonist holds a different view from your own. Remembering that negative politics can be in play, it will be vital to examine their motives and intent. Do you believe that they were well intentioned, or were they displaying some Machiavellian tendencies? Similarly, how would you describe their methods? Have they been honest and above board or gone about things in an underhand fashion? Is it cock-up or conspiracy; misunderstanding or malpractice? Or do they simply see things in a different way from how you see them? Factoring the political dimension into your analysis of the situation will help you to be savvy about the course of action you choose.

Remember too that conflicts often reflect aspects of the organization rather than differences between individuals. You feel that others are not maintaining standards or living the company values. Perhaps there's a problem arising from organizational structure, or roles are ambiguous. Either can cause people to stray – innocently – into areas where others consider they shouldn't be. In one situation, a manager in one department publicly blamed a peer in another for the breakdown of his marriage. It was actually a structural issue; there was overlap in their roles. They hated one another too, but that's another story!

Finally, what are the ramifications of the conflict? Have other people become involved? Has this had an adverse impact on your reputation? Has it set you back in your work? If so, resolving these spin-off issues will need to be a part of your plan.

To act or not to act …

Whilst conflict avoiders will *always* find reasons why they should not take action, there are legitimate circumstances in which it is appropriate not to tackle a particular issue. We will talk about some of these later in the chapter. However, it generally makes good sense at least to *attempt* to resolve conflicts as they arise, because of the inherent downsides of not doing so. These include:

> *Damage to you*: Bottling things up and worrying constantly about what people are thinking and saying about you are significant stressors. They can seriously damage your well-being – and your health. Swedish researchers from the University of Stockholm studied 2,755 male workers from the early 1990s to 2003. They asked the men how they coped with unfair treatment or conflict at work and took a range of measurements, including blood pressure, body

mass index and cholesterol levels. They recorded whether the workers used avoidance tactics, such as walking away from a situation, and whether they suffered headaches or other physical symptoms. After correcting for the degree of job strain the men were under, and biological factors, they found those who persistently bottled up their anger rather than expressing it openly were more than twice as likely to suffer from heart attacks or heart disease. These findings have been borne out in a range of studies. So you owe it to yourself to get issues out into the open and solve them.

Damage to others: This applies both to the individual, or individuals, involved in the conflict and to innocent bystanders. And sometimes the *perception* of conflict is enough to cause significant stress. Two close colleagues didn't speak for many months. They both had an opinion about why they weren't talking, but it was all based on a misunderstanding. By the time this became apparent, members of their teams had also fallen out, but there was no real conflict – the matter was sorted in 30 minutes by an impartial mediator.

Damage to the organization: Interpersonal conflicts of whatever nature will inevitably impact on the organization. Time wasted gossiping or back-stabbing is not productive. When this spirals out of control, negative politicking can have an adverse impact on profitability. Refusing to air problems perpetuates these clashes. The quality of work suffers, and customers may receive inconsistent and shoddy service. And acts of revenge can reach the public domain, causing reputational harm.

But if you're still unsure about whether to confront, there's a simple test: what will the impact be if this issue is *not* addressed?

- Will another person continue to perform in a suboptimal way – no matter how slight the shortcoming is?
- Will another person be disadvantaged personally?
- Will the organization suffer in any way – internally or externally?
- Will you continue to brood about the other person's actions?
- Will others feel bad?

If the answer to any of these questions is yes, then the problem needs to be addressed. And, if you're the right person to do it, then you need to act. If not, you will probably be best advised to keep your powder dry for the next flashpoint that *really* matters!

Plan your approach

Kenneth W Thomas and Ralph H Kilmann are leading authorities on conflict. They maintain that, in a conflict situation, you have a couple of basic decisions to make: how assertive to be and how cooperative to be. In their terminology, 'assertiveness' relates to the extent to which you want to 'win' the argument – or for your view to prevail. Cooperativeness is just the opposite – how happy you are for the other party to get what they want. Depending on your response to these two questions, you have five basic styles of conflict resolution to choose from. These are depicted in Figure 7.1.

FIGURE 7.1

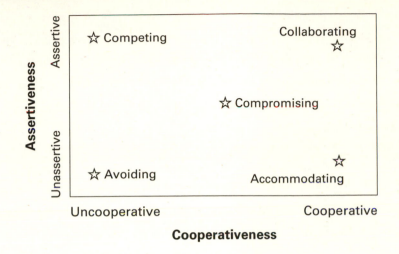

Conflict resolution styles

1. Competing

Competing is highly assertive but not at all cooperative. It is the style you would use when you want to win: for example, it might be appropriate in a situation where you know you're right (or at least strongly believe that you're right) or for issues you feel passionately about. You would also want to compete if the matter was a legal requirement or a moral dilemma. If you use this style, you could come across as being authoritative and directive – even dictatorial. Alternatively, it might be that you are so charismatic and influential – really selling the benefits – that, although technically you've 'won', the other person still walks away feeling good. Depending on how you choose to use this style, there is a risk that it can cause bad feeling and damage relationships, especially if you are the kind of person who competes naturally and frequently.

2. Collaborating

In the top right-hand corner, collaborating is both highly assertive and highly cooperative: the archetypal win–win style. This approach is suitable when the matter is important enough to warrant investing in the best possible outcome – and one which satisfies the key requirements of both parties. It may well be that, if the first person walks into the conflict wanting one solution and the second person wants another, having talked everything through they come up with a third solution together – one which meets all of their important criteria. Collaborating is a constructive approach to conflict. Too much of it, however, can be overly time consuming and wearing for others.

3. Compromising

Compromising is the middle ground. It's when you choose to strike a deal, a classic negotiation. You get some of what you want. So too does the other person. More rapid than collaborating, it is a pragmatic approach and therefore appropriate for less important matters. There is a risk, however, that you end up with neither party feeling quite satisfied with the eventual outcome.

4. Avoiding

Avoiding is neither assertive nor cooperative. As mentioned earlier in the chapter, however, an avoiding strategy can be appropriate in certain situations – when the matter is totally trivial, for example, or when it's likely to resolve itself. You might also wish to adopt an avoiding strategy when it would be more appropriate for someone else to deal with the issue. On occasions, while an avoiding strategy might not be the best approach, it may nevertheless be the only option available; there are times when a resolution is so unlikely that it's not even worth trying for. Some battles are just not worth fighting.

5. Accommodating

Accommodating is the opposite of competing – highly cooperative, but not assertive. It is the style you would adopt when you are happy for the other person to get their way; maybe the issue isn't important to you – or just a lot less important to you than it is to the other person. Alternatively, as you start to discuss the matter, you might realize that they have a point – their idea would actually work better than yours. Accommodating is also an appropriate style when the relationship with the other party is more important than the matter in hand. If you choose to accommodate, it usually makes sense to convey your flexibility and open-mindedness – and emphasize the fact that it's a one-off. This helps to ensure that you get the credit for accommodating, and will minimize the risk that your action sets an unfortunate precedent.

Horses for courses

According to Thomas and Kilmann, all these styles are appropriate at different times and in different circumstances. The trick is to know which to use, and to possess the skills to pull it off. In choosing your conflict resolution style, you always have to consider the personality of the other person and the nature of the conflict. The difficulty is that most people tend to use a couple of styles only, driven by their personality. For example, some might tend to inhabit the bottom half of the matrix; they are not very good at asserting their own requirements. This may be because they don't like to ask for favours, especially for themselves. Or they may just prefer it when other people get what they want. Contrast this individual with someone who habitually competes, occasionally collaborating when they believe their proposed solution could also incorporate the other person's wishes. This person is highly assertive; they are only cooperative when it won't diminish their own chance of winning.

Of course, there are many possible combinations, creating a diverse range of different individual profiles, some of which may appear to be contradictory. For example, it is quite common for someone to be highly competitive *and* highly avoidant. On the face of it, these strategies seem to be diametrically opposed; however, when you talk to people who fit this profile they are unsurprised, saying that when a conflict arises they quickly consider a) whether they can win, and b) whether they think it's worth the trouble. On the basis of the answers to these questions, they then decide whether to compete or avoid.

To establish your own preferences, you can use the 'Thomas–Kilmann Conflict Mode Instrument' (TKI). Further information is available at **http://www.opp.eu.com/psychometric_instruments/tki**. To give you a feel for your personal preferences, however, study the comments in Table 7.2. Which most accurately sum up your preferred approach to conflict?

If you mentally tick more statements in one section than in another, you are more likely to adopt that style of conflict resolution. As mentioned earlier, all five approaches are appropriate at times, but you need to understand when those times might be. Nine times out of ten, a naturally avoidant person can persuade themselves that 'best left unsaid' is the right strategy, whereas someone who is highly competitive will feel very strongly that they are right – and should therefore fight – in most situations. It is vital to be very honest with yourself and challenge your natural tendencies if you are to handle conflict situations well. Rigorously analysing each situation and sticking with the strategy that the analysis produces will help you to get it right.

TABLE 7.2

Competing

My way or the highway.

It's vitally important to win.

I know I'm right about this.

I am usually firm in pursuing my goals.

I am good at selling the merits and benefits of my approach to others.

Collaborating

Two heads are better than one.

Let's really explore the issues.

I try to use a problem-solving approach.

It's useful to seek the help and input of others in conflict situations.

Let's get all the issues into the open.

Compromising

Let's strike a deal.

Can we split the difference?

Let's find the middle ground.

I am happy to concede on some points if you do too.

It's important to be pragmatic about this.

Avoiding

I'll think about it tomorrow.

I hate confrontation.

It's not such a big deal.

I don't want to make a fuss about this.

There's no point even raising the issue.

Accommodating

It would be my pleasure.

It's obviously very important to you.

I often pander to other people's wishes.

I try not to hurt the other person's feelings.

It's often more important to preserve the relationship than win the argument.

Act!

Of course, a critical factor in deciding how to handle a conflict is your desired outcome: what *exactly* do you want to achieve? You must be clear about what this is before you enter into the debate. As well as your best-case scenario, you might also establish your fallback situation: what *would* you accept? Keeping this at the back of your mind as you engage with the other person will help to ensure you stay on track, no matter how much the conversation meanders.

Once you have established your outcome and which of the five broad approaches you wish to adopt, you need to think through what your process might be. For instance, a collaborative approach might look something like Figure 7.2:

FIGURE 7.2

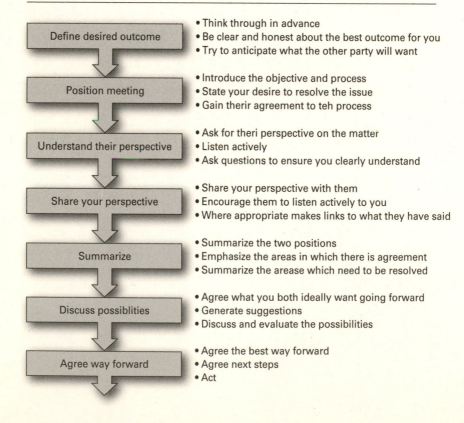

Define desired outcome
- Think through in advance
- Be clear and honest about the best outcome for you
- Try to anticipate what the other party will want

Position meeting
- Introduce the objective and process
- State your desire to resolve the issue
- Gain therir agreement to teh process

Understand their perspective
- Ask for theri perspective on the matter
- Listen actively
- Ask questions to ensure you clearly understand

Share your perspective
- Share your perspective with them
- Encourage them to listen actively to you
- Where appropriate makes links to what they have said

Summarize
- Summarize the two positions
- Emphasize the areas in which there is agreement
- Summarize the arease which need to be resolved

Discuss possiblities
- Agree what you both ideally want going forward
- Generate suggestions
- Discuss and evaluate the possibilities

Agree way forward
- Agree the best way forward
- Agree next steps
- Act

Again, you might deviate from this, but understanding how you plan to achieve your desired outcome will give you a good starting framework for the meeting.

The second box describes how you position your meeting. This is critical. If you go in with an attack, implying that they are the ones with the problem and they have to change, this is unlikely to instil a collaborative mindset in the other person. If, by contrast, you acknowledge there have been some issues between the two of you and say that you are keen to work out a way of operating for the future that will be more productive, it suggests more of a two-way process – and shared responsibility. Getting the meeting off on the right footing is absolutely vital. Do your best to see things from the other person's perspective. Knowing what you know about them, what is likely to encourage them to be receptive, honest and constructive with you?

You then need to think about how to give them the feedback. Try to avoid falling into common traps such as being judgemental or using emotive language.

But how *should* it be done? Below are some tips to bear in mind when you have bad news to give:

- Be really *specific* about what exactly it is you think the person should be doing differently. Otherwise there's a real danger that your observations will be heard as 'I don't like you as a person' rather than 'I think you should do or have done this differently.'

- Make sure the time and place are appropriate. Never criticize people in public – it is humiliating for them; choose a private room away from the rest of the team where you can both talk openly about the issue.

- Where possible, don't delay. While you occasionally need to give yourself a few minutes – or hours – to calm down, you shouldn't put off the moment for too long. It is not helpful to haul someone over the coals for an incident that happened six months ago. Nor is it best practice to allow destructive behaviour to continue for years without talking to the individual about it.

- Put the effort in – give it the importance it deserves and prepare properly. Even 10 minutes' preparation – on the message you want to give, the impact you want to have and the way in which you should tackle the issue – can make all the difference to an encounter.

- Anticipate the response – how can you make the message more palatable without undermining its impact?

- Balance positive and negative feedback.

- Deliver negative feedback in a non-critical way. If possible, depersonalize the issue: talk about a specific piece of work rather than make blanket statements about the individual. Set it in context – particularly flagging up where the destructive behaviour or poor performance seemed out of character. Be sensitive. Give appropriate examples.

- Concentrate on pitch and tone so valuable information is not seen as a complaint, criticism, moan or nag.

- Beware of being patronizing.

- Remember throughout that you want to solve the problem.

Helping someone solve a problem is very closely aligned with the art of influence and persuasion – you need to adopt different approaches with different people. It may be useful, therefore, to refer back to the previous chapter as a part of your preparation. This will help you to be clear about the type of person you are dealing with and the nature of the situation.

Chapter Eight
Dealing with relationship breakdown

Four out of five people believe that people need to collaborate at work – and the more savvy they are, the more likely they are to hold this view. Two-thirds agree that it's not what you know but who you know. Over half say that people get emotionally involved with one another and 41 per cent believe that it helps to have a best friend at work. Interestingly, on these last two points, men are almost 50 per cent more likely to feel this way than women. So relationships at work matter massively, as does their breakdown: every single person we interviewed as part of the research referred to this situation without prompting.

Why do you want good working relationships?

Robust working relationships are not merely a 'nice to have'. There are few jobs in which there is no need to forge and maintain strong links – at the very least with colleagues and the boss. But in some roles, people find themselves reconciling the needs of customers, suppliers, other stakeholders – and even the world at large. Our research clearly indicates that a work environment where people positively respect rather than merely tolerate each other makes them not just happier and more satisfied at work, but also more productive and committed. And possibly now more than ever before, since networking is accepted as one of the most critical skills in business, while technology enables people to keep in touch with a far wider range of contacts, instantaneously. As one senior executive put it, 'Strong working relationships oil the machine!'

By contrast, when relationships break down, this can cause anxiety, aggressiveness and hostility. Factions form. And a great deal of time is wasted on the bitching and back-stabbing that disputes spawn. In our research, almost everyone we interviewed had experienced a relationship failure at one time or another. For many, the problems were ongoing. A surprising number had chosen to leave the organization rather than continue to do battle on a daily basis – though most later regretted not having engaged more actively with the politics of the situation and done more to repair the relationship.

So, to be savvy, you need the ability to forge strong links with a wide range of different types of people. And you also need to be able to spot potential problems and deal with them as they arise – early and effectively. Unfortunately, the whole notion of productive working relationships is often misunderstood, both in terms of what they are and how to develop them. This chapter aims to demystify the art of relationship building and outline what to do when things go wrong.

What is a good working relationship?

Whilst many people believe that success in business is significantly related to the ability to build good working relationships, there are still a surprising number who think it's all about drinks at the pub and being intimately acquainted with the details of other people's personal lives. In fact, it's not necessary to go 'extracurricular' to develop a good working relationship. You must, however, understand that its essence lies in establishing a win–win situation rather than one person profiting from the other's failure. Critical ingredients include: respect, trust, listening and empathy, with an emphasis on working together to get the most from combined strengths. This can be challenging – some of the most powerful relationships are those forged between individuals who are quite different from one another. Rather than sharing the same thoughts and values, they complement one another's strengths, compensate for each other's weaknesses and bring such completely different perspectives to bear on a situation that their analysis of it tends to be richer and better judged than one produced by a more homogeneous pairing. However, opposites are also liable to rub each other up the wrong way. Forging effective relationships requires you to get beyond the irritation factor and really make something of personal differences. Recognizing the need to consider alternative approaches to your own is a starting point. But it's not enough. You need to be able to value different styles and reach the position where you can exploit your *collective* strengths to achieve company goals. For instance, a thorough, methodical worker may be intolerable to a fast-moving, target-driven type. However, the former's strengths can be put to good use in averting a disaster caused by an ill-thought-through strategy.

Win–win

There are many roles which, on the face of it, appear to have inbuilt conflicts; they seem to operate on a win–lose basis. But if this were the case, what would be the point of the relationship? Examples include the tension between the sales or business development side and the people who develop a service or manufacture the product. To bring in the deal, salespeople sometimes resort to underpricing and/or overpromising. This clearly makes it difficult for those who are responsible for the delivery – and can compromise profit. Similar conflicts tend to arise in IT (development vs maintenance), compliance and risk management (mitigating risk vs capitalizing on opportunities) – and between many other natural enemies. So where's the win–win? To find it, you have to identify a higher purpose. For example, both systems developers and those who maintain the technology are there to ensure that the company has IT that is fit for purpose and reliable. The salespeople and the delivery people need to collaborate to ensure that both top and bottom lines are in line with the organization's targets. And compliance exists to ensure that the business strikes the right balance between being commercial and being legally secure. Whilst there are bound to be everyday frustrations, there is a win–win if you view the situation strategically enough, from a corporate rather than a departmental or individual perspective.

Elsewhere, the win–win is often more obvious and it's much easier to be collaborative, cooperative and even collegial. And of course, working relationships don't need to reflect the formal design of the organization. Some of the most effective networking involves people who see mutual benefit from having a relationship that would not show up in an organization chart.

Respect

Mutual respect is a fundamental aspect of effective working relationships and a great deal of research has been conducted into what creates it. The answer is unsurprising: mutuality is the key. If you genuinely respect others, the chances are that they will reciprocate. By putting this simple principle into practice, many people have transformed both the way they feel about others and the way they feel about themselves, just by making a concerted effort to value the contribution of colleagues. But how do you develop respect for an individual if it doesn't occur automatically? First, you need to get to know them. Engage them in a dialogue and really listen. Why do they do what they do? What drives and motivates them? Then evaluate the value they add. If you can't see it, talk to someone who appears to have a more positive perception of the person. Assess the benefits of their strengths. Consider whether the negatives could be the inevitable downside of the positives – remember we all have weaknesses! Give them the benefit of the doubt.

And what if you've done all this and you still can't find a basis for respecting a particular individual? It's perhaps a controversial view, but I believe you are only entitled to adopt this position where you suspect the other person to be unethical – a Machiavellian or a Barbarian. If this is not the case, you have one of two paths available to you: either find something to admire in them as described above, or take the trouble to give them feedback about their performance or behaviour. Prepare your case carefully, be clear about what you want to achieve (it's not enough to dump the information on the individual; you must have a positive outcome in mind) and make sure you listen to their point of view: remember that you're hoping to find a reason to raise your opinion of them, not to confirm your reservations. So they must be given the benefit of any vestiges of doubt that remain.

Trust

Another important cornerstone of effective relationships is that of trust: to work together, it is vital that you have trust in others and they in you. Without this, people become suspicious, nervous, demotivated and sometimes paranoid. They can spend a lot of time checking things out and covering their tracks.

So how do you develop trust? There is a school of thought which believes that trust is binary: you either have it or you don't. And some say that, once broken, it can never be regained. A percentage of the population trust immediately – they find it easy – and it's only when that trust is proven to have been misplaced that it breaks down. Others take a long time to develop it, being naturally more cautious. But regardless of your personality type, trust tends to breed trust: as with respect, if you trust others, the chances are they will trust you.

But you also need to be consistent, both in terms of how you deal with people and in 'walking the talk'. If you say something is important, you must act accordingly – otherwise people will accuse you of paying lip service. If you are confided in, you must respect that confidentiality. You should not talk about others behind their backs. And you need to deliver what you promise. If you do all this, you will demonstrate yourself to be trustworthy.

But what about trusting others? Clearly, if they do all of the above, you are more likely to consider them honourable and honest. If they don't, it is vitally important to understand whether they are well intentioned but naive, or if their motives are suspect, ie someone with Machiavellian or Barbarian tendencies. It's a very sensitive area: no one appreciates being told that they are perceived to be untrustworthy. But if you are dealing with someone who is positively motivated, you owe it to them (and ultimately to yourself) to let them know what impression they are conveying by their behaviour. They can then choose whether to change or not. The Machiavellian or Barbarian is an altogether different proposition: it is imprudent to trust them and – unless they change – your relationship with them must be a wary one.

Listening

Listening was covered in depth in Chapter 6. It is, of course, also one of the fundamentals both of being savvy and of developing effective relationships: how can you hope to foster a relationship with someone if you don't know what they think or feel about things? Listen carefully and patiently. Listen for feelings and emotions, as well as for facts and information. Demonstrate you've listened by summarizing and checking your understanding. Many people *are* listening but don't appear to be, because they miss out this vital element of the process. And respond to what the other person is saying. That doesn't mean you always have to agree with them but it does mean sharing your own feelings and thoughts on an issue.

Empathy

Empathy is the art of being able to put yourself in the shoes of another person and to understand the way they feel about things. It's about seeing their perspective and being on their side. And it's about striking up rapport. You may feel that you can't possibly empathize unless you yourself have gone through a similar experience. But that's not the case. You just need to be able to use your imagination without making what might be false assumptions. How do you do this? Well, careful questioning is one important aspect – asking the other person what they think about a situation and what the solution might be, rather than imposing your own views. And, of course, the ability to listen to the response is fundamental here as well. Paying close attention to body language, pace and mood is also key. Jollying someone along and trying to share your own enthusiasm will do little to enhance the frame of mind of someone who is feeling really down. Matching their style and pace, without mimicking the individual, will help far more and is likely to be more effective. If appropriate, you can then start to raise your energy levels and inject some positivity – but it's critical to do this very gradually.

So much for effective working relationships. They can sometimes be difficult to build, but the payoff should justify the investment. You may also regard some colleagues as personal friends, but this is not essential; there's nothing to stop you having a perfectly adequate working relationship with someone you don't consider to be a personal friend.

What happens when relationships break down?

Just as good relationships contribute to the welfare of an organization, relationship breakdowns usually cause problems.

Take an extreme example. If you have a chairman and a chief executive who can't bear to be in the same room as each other, what chance do you have of developing an effective corporate strategy? It's impossible to keep a lid on this sort of situation. Employees, customers and other stakeholders will soon be talking about it, and it won't be long before the analysts and journalists pick up the story. As a result, confidence in the organization plummets. Less dramatic, but still damaging, are rifts between managers of departments or team leaders. Lack of cooperation, backbiting and blame are all symptoms and a lose–lose situation can quickly emerge – especially when people spend more time trying to make sure that they're not held accountable for failures than they do attempting to rectify matters. And this can become quite extreme. One of the people we interviewed talked about how all the management information used to judge performance in their organization was skewed to ensure that one department was not blamed for the problems.

The complete breakdown of any relationship between two people who need to work together – no matter where they sit in the company – will have a negative impact on the business. However, the corporate impact can pale into insignificance compared with the personal impact. At the lower end of the damage scale, you find people looking for other jobs. As you move up the scale you find stress, illness – and worse. No one wants to have enemies. No one wants to agonize for hours about how to avoid coming into contact with someone. No one wants to feel paranoid about what another person could be saying about them. So the problem of relationship breakdown needs to be addressed.

What causes meltdowns?

Like many people-related issues, diagnosis of the cause and formulation of a solution is not straightforward. There can be all sorts of reasons why people don't get on. For example:

- *Chemistry* – 'I don't like you.'
- *Behaviour/style* – 'I don't like the way you do things.'
- *Philosophy/values* – 'I don't like what you stand for.'
- *Conflict of interest* – 'I will work to prevent you being successful, because a gain for you inevitably produces a loss for me.'
- *Injury* – 'I don't like what you did.'
- *Prejudice* – 'I don't like your type of person.'
- *Jealousy* – 'I don't like you for what you've got.'

How to deal with breakdowns

As there are a number of different *causes* of relationship breakdown, there are also many different types of *solution*.

Outlined below are some strategies which you can use to help mend broken relationships. Under each category is a case study, followed by two sets of guidelines: the first is appropriate if you *personally* are involved in the breakdown; the second is designed for dealing with situations in which *other people* are involved, which is particularly relevant for those in a managerial position.

1. Chemistry

CASE STUDY

'It was clear they would never get on as soon as they clapped eyes on one another.' These were the words of one director, recalling the first meeting of Paul and Roberta. Paul had just been recruited as the company actuary and Roberta was responsible for marketing. She had not been involved in the interviewing process. Nor had she met Paul until the first executive team meeting – and, since others had, she was probably feeling somewhat aggrieved about this. Roberta was an outgoing, flamboyant character, whilst Paul was more thoughtful and quiet. She developed a habit of putting Paul on the spot, which placed him firmly outside his comfort zone and he didn't respond too well. This served to lessen her already low opinion of him. Colleagues took Roberta to one side and advised her to ease off, but to no avail, until, during one conversation, Roberta realized why she had developed such an aversion to Paul. She had a real problem with anyone who came across like a schoolteacher. Paul's style was definitely pedantic, and to make matters worse, he actually bore a physical resemblance to a lecturer she had fallen out with at university! Once she realized this, she made a concerted effort to change her approach with Paul. She decided to explain the situation to him and to apologize for her behaviour. They never became bosom buddies but they did develop a productive working relationship that was based on mutual respect for the other's differences.

And in terms of what to do about it?

When it's you ...

Chemistry is possibly one of the most difficult problems to deal with as it's not based on rational thought. The chances are you didn't like this person the moment you clapped eyes on them. So how are you going to change that? First of all, challenge your assumption that the problem is chemistry alone. Has something happened that has created resentment on your part? Or is it the way they approach a task that drives you crazy? If you can't identify a specific cause, then it may just be chemistry. Question: do they also think there's a problem? If so, you will need to speak to them. Conflict is never easy – and it's anathema to some people – but it can be made slightly more palatable if tackled in a constructive way (see Chapter 7). Think through what they're like and plan to tackle the conversation in a way that is more likely to appeal to them. Be open about the problem and seek their view. Just having the conversation could help.

If you don't think the other person is aware of the problem, then you don't necessarily need to have the discussion. Instead, convince yourself that you *can* get on with the individual. Find something to value about them, make an active effort to like them, and then treat them with the respect they deserve as a human being. Of course, it is far easier said than done, but if you succeed, you'll feel better not only about the relationship but also about yourself.

When it's others ...

If this is a problem you need to sort out in others, you must help them realize the damage they're causing – quickly! Tackle each individual separately first. Give them the feedback, outline the impact and explore the reasons for their behaviour. If the problem continues, it may be necessary to talk to them together, in private. Use mediation skills to try to bring the two together, and once you've started to get movement, it may be desirable to set them a joint task. You need to be convinced that they want to make it work, otherwise the results could be disastrous. Start with a small project and give a very clear brief, so that there's no scope for fighting over how the task should be approached. Review progress. Then it may be safe to give them shared responsibility for an important, difficult project. Send them on a business trip, for instance, or make them jointly responsible for planning a training session. Time in each other's company can work wonders. The main aim is to encourage them to recognize their inter-dependence by creating shared objectives, a common enemy or a situation in which they must sink or swim together.

2. Behaviour/style

CASE STUDY

Two colleagues collaborated on new product development. Benedict was thoughtful, introverted and prone to procrastination, seeking always the space and time to think things through. He loathed public brainstorming sessions, preferring quiet reflection on his own. The other, James, was far more outgoing and hated indecision. He felt as though his ideas were disregarded and undervalued – 'They just disappear into a black hole, so what's the point?' James complained that they never seemed to launch anything, or, by the time they did, they'd already missed the boat. He did confess, however, to being somewhat impetuous and, on occasion, failing to evaluate ideas properly. At an offsite session, they did some personality profiling and, for the first time, realized just how different they were. Part of the session involved time for colleagues to establish how their approaches might work more effectively together. Benedict and James agreed on a process which enabled them to compromise and get the most from their skills and strengths. They also found that the personality profile gave them a common language which enabled them to laugh at the other's foibles and took the edge off any mutual frustration.

And in terms of what to do about it?

When it's you ...

Organizations populated by clones lack the variety needed to be successful. You need to have a rich blend of different styles, skills and strengths. Unfortunately, differences are not always easily tolerated. The important thing here is to understand a particular difference and its value, then make sure you are maximizing it to realize joint potential. It is not always evident precisely what the difference is; you may need help in articulating it. Talk to the person about your feelings and encourage them to give you feedback. Be honest, not only in describing how you see their behaviour but also in the impact that it has on you. Discuss each other's strengths, reach an understanding of how they can be used and agree how you will work together in the future. You may need assistance from an objective third party to help you see things from the other's perspective.

When it's others ...

When you see others clashing in this way, you may need to intervene to help each recognize the other's contribution. Give them feedback. Get them to give each other feedback. Use an impartial mediator if necessary. And perhaps do some profiling with them, as in the case study. Ultimately, the individuals involved must learn how to deal with each other and how to interpret what is being said in an emotional language that is not their own.

3. Philosophy/values

CASE STUDY

A world-leading expert and academic was engaged to work in a manufacturing company to help them with their production. This individual, Monica, firmly believed in things being 100 per cent right – and was very direct with colleagues when she thought they were cutting corners or being lazy. When they said it would take six weeks to do something, she would prove them wrong by completing the task in 48 hours. Fundamentally, she didn't really think they were clever or experienced enough. Her colleagues acknowledged that she was often right, but felt that she would get a better result by working collaboratively with them, rather than – as they perceived it – trying to make them look stupid. They also maintained that Monica did not demonstrate the political savvy required to work in industry – her approach was more suited to an academic environment. This caused such ripples across the company that restructuring and a re-evaluation of her role and authority levels were required in order to create a tolerable way of working.

And in terms of what to do about it?

When it's you ...

This is difficult. Values and beliefs go right to the very centre of an individual's character; you are not going to change that. Nor are you likely to change your own to fit more neatly with their philosophy. Why would you want to, even if you could? All you can do is recognize the difference, believe with all your heart that they have just as much right to their values as you do to yours, and get on with getting on with them. You can then work with the person to agree how you should both modify your behaviours, so that you can work more productively (see 2. Behaviour/style above).

This becomes a different issue if one person is 'right' and the other is 'wrong'. For instance, it may well be that you hold a set of beliefs which is consistent with what the organization is striving for, while the other person clearly does not. When this is the case, it is often possible to point out instances when the 'offender' has acted inappropriately and say why you think their behaviour was out of line. Talk to the individual – tell them your views. If that doesn't work, there may be merit in enlisting the support of your boss. Outline your case carefully, give examples to back it up, and state how you have tried to address the situation. Be objective and avoid exaggeration.

When it's others ...

If you are called in to deal with an issue like this, it's essential to be impartial. More often than not, both philosophies are acceptable to the company – just not to the individuals involved! Here you have to look for common ground. What is it that they both agree on? Can this form the basis of a productive working relationship? Point out to them that people do have different values: one person might throw heart and soul into getting to the top, while the other wants a more balanced lifestyle. These differences need to be accommodated – by the organization and by the individuals involved – if both are going to continue working for the company. Get them to think of ways in which they can plan and organize their work to get the most from each other. Then follow up and review the situation.

4. Conflict of interest

CASE STUDY

Ahmed was in compliance. Part of his job involved telling people that they couldn't do the things they wanted to do. Most colleagues accepted this – and recognized that he was just acting in the interests of the organization – but one team, headed by Steve, not only seemed unwilling to take 'no' for an answer, but also seemed intent on undermining Ahmed's reputation. They accused him of being negative, unconstructive and nit-picking. They felt that he should have been more focused on enabling them to achieve their goals, rather than telling them why they weren't able to. Ahmed started to avoid Steve's team and even became panicked when they sent him an e-mail. He lost confidence, which started to impact on the way he handled other internal clients. Eventually, he was moved to another part of compliance and a colleague took his role. Steve didn't give Ahmed's successor any easier a ride; there was an inbuilt tension, which others accepted, but Steve didn't.

And in terms of what to do about it?

When it's you ...

Frequently, with this type of conflict, the issue involved is organizational, not personal. In other words, the problem is caused by structure and process – not individual differences: the way things are currently set up, people can't help but compete. Project managers fighting for funding from a limited pot, for instance, or remuneration policies which reward individual performance but fail to take into account cross-selling. The solution here is one of compromise and 'swings and roundabouts'. Until the systems or processes change, the conflict will remain. So it's in your interest to talk to the individual concerned and agree how best you can work around the problems. Remind them it's not personal, be open about the potential win–lose situation, and stress your desire for a compromise that is acceptable to both of you.

When it's others ...

If you are charged with dealing with this type of breakdown, it could well be that you are talking about one team vs another. Of course, the ideal situation is to change the system, eg by adjusting reward mechanisms, so that people benefit from cooperating instead of competing. In some large corporates, a significant proportion of the bonus paid to an individual senior manager is tied to their delivering projects which benefit other departments. If this sort of arrangement is not practically possible, it is necessary to alter the way they perceive the situation. Remind them of the principle of 'you scratch my back, I'll scratch yours.' Make them understand that cooperation is valued by the organization; it will be recognized – and ultimately rewarded – even if there is disappointment in the short term. Then be true to your word.

But often, there is a deeper conflict, which can't be removed by a change in the system. For example, the team responsible for maintaining computers will always hanker after stability, while those who design systems will always want change. Help each to understand the problems the other faces. Get them working together, focusing on higher-level objectives and goals. Remind them that they are both needed. Beware of false dilemmas – the black-and-white thinking which leads us to insist on 'either/or' solutions, when nine times out of ten compromise is possible – and necessary.

5. Injury

CASE STUDY

Lily, a manager in the leisure sector, had had a series of issues with Fatima, her new boss. Then one day Lily was shown an e-mail that had been sent by Fatima to the whole of Lily's team. Not only did it imply criticism of Lily, but it also undermined her authority – why was the boss circumnavigating her with instructions for her team, and not even copying her? So the e-mail was damning in itself. But when her team members scrolled down, they discovered an e-mail chain, which made matters far worse. Fatima had e-mailed senior members of the executive, complaining that Lily was not fit to do her job, was underperforming and that they should think about getting rid of her. All objective measures indicated otherwise: Lily had built her part of the business up from scratch and was hitting targets, both financial and customer satisfaction. She was doing well *despite* the arrival of her new boss. Allegations followed. Lily was accused of poor team management, failing to fulfil a number of key tasks (even though these tasks were actually within Fatima's remit), cheating on timesheets and being weak. Lily was signed off by her doctor for stress and has since left the organization, bringing a successful case against the company for unfair dismissal. Fatima is still there – and is incidentally a personal friend of the owner – but that part of the business is now failing.

And in terms of what to do about it?

When it's you ...

If an individual has upset or hurt you, allowing it to fester will only store up trouble. You owe it to yourself to tell someone about it. The best person to talk to, if you can face it, is the person who caused the problem. The culprit may not realize they have done anything wrong, in which case just airing your views can clear up misunderstandings. However, they may be well aware of what they've done – and think they have a good reason for it. You need to know what that is. If you really can't face confronting the individual, then you should talk to your manager about the situation and enlist their support. (If it's your manager who's hurt you, see Chapter 9, 'Managing your boss', for advice.)

When it's others ...

If you are that manager – or you happen to be a friend who cares about what's happened and would like to help sort it out – you need to get to both parties quickly, otherwise the situation will deteriorate. There are nearly always two sides to a story. Both need to be out in the open. You could think about using an objective mediator – someone without an axe to grind. Explain carefully what the issues are. Let each person have their say and make the other listen. Allow them to talk it through. Summarize throughout. Then get them to come to some agreement on how to work together in the future. Make sure they know that you're going to follow this up. The ultimate aim here is to get people to forgive and forget – and ensure it doesn't happen again.

6. Prejudice

CASE STUDY

An assistant director, Geoff, in a not-for-profit organization reported that senior management was becoming more and more dominated by women. All the new hires were female – and seemed to be a particular 'type'. They held different values and openly rubbished anyone who had been at the organization for any length of time, on the basis that they were 'old school'. There was a restructuring, which removed a number of posts at the assistant director level. The recruitment process which followed was not perceived to be fair. A valued peer – who happened to be both male and black – was thought to have been treated appallingly and found himself without a role. Rumour had it that he had been discriminated against, on the grounds of race, gender – and being perceived to be 'old school'. The assistant directors who remained in post said that they had lost faith in the new regime and found it immensely difficult to engage with the senior management team whom they considered had practised discrimination.

And in terms of what to do about it?

When it's you …

Prejudice is a word that is often used to describe a range of feelings and emotions connected to fear and dislike of individuals who are different from us, or who don't fit into our idea of the norm. A prejudice is an unreasonable judgement based on little knowledge or experience of the individual or group of people concerned. Prejudices become harmful when they form the basis for negative action or behaviour against people. This then develops into discrimination – treating others unfairly because of something about themselves they cannot change, or that others dislike – often irrationally.

In an organizational context, discrimination can occur in all kinds of areas, for many different reasons; traditionally we are aware of discrimination related to gender, race, sexual orientation and religion. Wider issues, such as age, class, geographical background, political allegiances and social status, are also reasons why people discriminate negatively. Regardless of the issue, discrimination in the workplace should not be tolerated.

Discrimination normally takes three forms:

- direct behaviour aimed at an individual specifically because of their sex, race, disability or other grounds;
- indirect systems, procedures, requirements or conditions which – whether intentional or not – have the impact of discriminating against another person on the grounds described above;
- victimization – further action against a person because they have already made a complaint.

So what can you do if you feel you've been discriminated against? Talking to someone you can trust about your experience can help you focus on the type of action that you wish to take. There are several choices:

- Assertively challenge the perpetrator yourself.
- Ask a friend or colleague to help you confront the behaviour.
- Report the matter to your line manager or HR department.
- Ask your union to intervene on your behalf.
- Seek legal advice.

Whatever your choice of action, no one needs to put up with discriminatory behaviour and organizations have a legal and moral responsibility to ensure we all work in a safe, positive environment.

When it's others ...

This is perhaps the most tricky area. Prejudice is difficult both to prove and to deal with. But it's essential to be alert to this type of conflict – especially as a manager – or you could find yourself with a lawsuit on your hands. Tread carefully. Explain how it appears to you – and to the other people involved – using examples to back up your case. Listen and explore. Make it clear that you won't tolerate discrimination on any grounds. Remind people of the law and company policy. Say that you will be seeking feedback to see how the situation develops – from them, from the person who has drawn your attention to the situation, and from others who are in a position to observe what is happening. Then keep a close eye on things. The aim here is to generate (or impose) understanding and tolerance. It's not easy and it doesn't happen overnight. But exposing the problem can certainly speed this process up.

7. Jealousy

CASE STUDY

A communications manager, Charles, was jealous of the relationship which a female colleague, Claire, had with the senior partner in the firm where they worked. Claire had travelled with the senior partner. She had successfully helped him design and run critical meetings and conferences. She had also enabled him to communicate effectively in times of terrible turmoil. Jealousy drove Charles to rubbish his colleague behind her back. He tried to cut her out of critical meetings and withheld as much information as possible. He did his best to match the closeness of her relationship with the senior partner, booking as many meetings as he could – and then not sharing what was discussed with Claire. Fortunately, in the eyes of the senior partner, Claire was undamaged by this campaign; her relationship with him was too strong and the value he knew she added was too great. But tensions between the two colleagues worsened. They eventually reached a position where it became impossible for them to work with one another.

And in terms of what to do about it?

When it's you ...

This too is a difficult area, since most people who are jealous of others will find all sorts of alternative explanations for their aversion. So the first thing you need to do is to acknowledge the real cause of your feelings. Remember that jealousy is a natural emotion and many people experience it. But at the same time be determined to do something about it. What precisely are you envious of? Why? It's worth remembering that you have strengths too. Others could well be jealous of those. Tell your-self that this negative emotion is just not worthy of you. It is unlikely to benefit you and may well damage your reputation.

You may not be able to find it in yourself to wish the other person well, but you probably can pull back from being actively – and pointlessly – competitive.

But what if someone else is jealous of you? In this circumstance, the solution will depend on the source of the jealousy and the way in which it is manifesting itself in the other's behaviour. Inclusion and involvement can sometimes be the best remedy; if the jealous party is brought more into your sphere of operation, this can help to reduce their envy. Failing that, just building a better relationship with the person will make them feel included – and perhaps believe that some of your positive press will rub off on them!

When it's others ...

If you have to deal with what you suspect to be jealousy in another person, explore it carefully with them. Try to get to the root cause. Remember that insecurity can cause these feelings, so make sure you let them know how much you value their strengths. Tell them that you consider them to be too good a performer and too much of an asset to allow jealousy to get in their way. Point out how much better they would be if they could conquer these undermining, unconstructive thoughts.

What are the principles for dealing with breakdowns?

You can try to bypass a conflict: it's sometimes possible to arrange things so that the people who are at loggerheads never have to deal with each other. However, this is a laborious and hazardous approach, which leads to inefficiency and distraction. Innocent bystanders get involved, and of course, the basic problem remains. So it's far better to deal with the situation.

Ideally you would be able to foresee potential clashes and avoid them. However, without prescience it's inevitable that personal conflicts will arise from time to time. Here are some basic rules of thumb for dealing with them:

- *Nip trouble in the bud.* Don't allow the situation to deteriorate by ignoring it and hoping it'll go away – ie 'kicking the can down the road'. The longer a dispute continues, the more difficult and painful it becomes to implement an effective solution.

- *Use an honest broker.* People usually work through their problems faster with third-party assistance. They may need help in getting the other person to listen or to understand how their own behaviour is coming across.

- *Don't rush to judgement.* The blame is rarely all on one side. It's important that someone understands both sides of the story.

- *Assume the best motives.* It's very easy to assume that people are deliberately being difficult and obstructive. Unless you know it to be untrue, do your best to believe that both individuals mean well and that they are not digging their heels in for no reason at all.

- *Understand the reasons.* Don't waste time picking off symptoms; the issues will just re-emerge in a different way. Take time to get to the heart of the matter.

- *Make the remedy fit the cause.* Choose an appropriate and proportionate way of dealing with the problem.

- *Follow-up.* This needs to happen regularly and over time. It's vital to prevent old wounds reopening or hostilities resuming after an official ceasefire has been declared.

To end ...

Prejudice is clearly one of the reasons why working relationships break down. But how common is it? Our survey identified that around 60 per cent believe that their organizations do not discriminate: 60 per cent state that men and women have equal opportunities; 61 per cent say the same of ethnic minorities; 62 per cent disagree with the statement that homosexuality could adversely affect an individual's career; while 62 per cent disagree with the statement that there is a reluctance to recruit women of childbearing age. Of course, this does not mean that the remaining c.40 per cent believe there is discrimination; many were undecided or unprepared to answer. However, of those who did, almost a quarter said they believe women do not enjoy equal opportunities, 17 per cent observed discrimination on the grounds of ethnicity and 15 per cent on the grounds of homosexuality. These percentages are still unacceptably high.

Chapter Nine
Managing your boss

When we interviewed people about politics in their organizations, one of the most significant causes of perceived negative politicking was a difficult relationship with the boss. Whether commenting on ill treatment, lack of respect, incompetence or jealousy, people were clear about the impact: conflict with the boss is stressful in the extreme. And if you work for a woman, watch out: our quantitative research findings indicate that 60 per cent of people believe they are more likely to fall out with a female boss than with a male boss (only 5 per cent think you are more likely to fall out with a male boss). Our survey also shows that only two-thirds of people actually respect their bosses, and these are more likely to be people who self-score as being politically savvy. Interestingly, a higher percentage – 71 per cent – considers that their boss respects them! Only 18 per cent feel patronized by their boss, but a massive 50 per cent of people believe that their boss has favourites. Women come off badly here again; those with a female boss are 50 per cent more likely to perceive that she has favourites.

Why are good relationships with your boss critical?

Regardless of what you do, where you work or the level you're at, your relationship with your boss is the most critical one you have in your professional life. Bosses can fulfil a wide range of different roles. They can educate, guide and challenge. They can promote and support your career. And they can make the difference between a fulfilling, productive – and satisfied – working life and a stress-filled, disheartening and miserable time. What more powerful demonstration of savvy could there be than a successful relationship with your boss, which you maintain effectively – by dealing with any problems as soon as they arise, if not before!

What can a boss do for you?

Let's just take a while to review what a good boss might be doing for you – why it's so important to get them on side. Amongst the roles they fulfil are:

- mentor and coach;
- advocate;
- role model;
- teacher;
- sounding board;
- confidant;
- mirror.

Mentor and coach

Good bosses will help you to understand how to be successful in your current role and beyond. They will ensure that you know what to do and how to conduct yourself at all times. Through coaching, they will guide you to your own solutions – ones which work for you. And through their wise words, they will help you to appreciate the nuances of the culture and learn what the acceptable behaviours are. Ultimately, they will assist you in achieving your potential, which may well mean promoting you beyond their own level.

Advocate

Linked with this, your boss can be an advocate for you, as well as a champion of your development. In many organizations, promotion will depend on the staunch and credible support of the line manager. Clearly, it will help if the boss is a Star – with sway and influence in the organization. Not so good if the boss is a Barbarian – not that such bosses are likely to be singing your praises anyway!

Role model

The lasting influence that a boss has on an individual – and their working lives – is phenomenal. People often talk about powerful role models decades later. Clearly, when you are looking for tips, tactics and guidance in terms of how to approach things, and even what makes for a positive, productive mindset, your boss is often the first port of call. Observing the boss, seeing how they handle things and emulating their behaviour is of paramount importance in the development of anyone at work.

Teacher

Teaching is slightly different from mentoring and coaching. It relates more to the technical aspects of your work – learning the ropes. A good teacher can help you to acquire knowledge and experience. They can point you in the right direction when you need information. They look after your practical development and help you to identify shortcomings in your skills and expertise.

Sounding board

As a sounding board, your boss should be available for you to discuss ideas with and a source of feedback which is open, honest and challenging. They will expect you to have thought things through before you approach them, but once you have, they should be willing to critique your ideas robustly.

Confidant

A boss may also be a confidant – a supportive listener and advisor. They can help you to work through problems, particularly those of a personal nature. A good manager recognizes that emotional issues do not arise only in your home life but that the emotional dimension is a critical aspect of your work too – how to handle people that you perceive to be difficult, enhancing your influence and building your confidence, to name but a few. But be careful: busy bosses can be overwhelmed by the emotional outpourings of people who have come to view them as a crutch but whom they perceive as weaker than colleagues who make fewer demands on their time.

Mirror

Implicit within each of these roles is feedback. A boss cannot be a good manager unless they hold the mirror up to you on a regular basis. Limiting it to the formal annual appraisal process is no longer acceptable. Feedback has to be frequent, ongoing – and, of course, constructive.

How do you manage your boss?

Ideally, you get things off to a good start – being on the back foot and having to deal with problems that have arisen because you haven't managed your boss well is not a good place to be. So, how do you do this? There are 10 golden rules:

1 Understand what they require from you and how they like to work.

2 Be proactive.

3 Help them to achieve their business objectives.

4 Don't ask questions you could answer yourself.

5 Be straight and make your apologies count.

6 Don't react emotionally.

7 Go beyond the call of duty.

8 Don't insult your boss's intelligence.

9 Ask for and give feedback.

10 Don't get a reputation for being a whinger.

Understand what they require from you and how they like to work

It is remarkable how few people ask these critical questions of their boss. And then they're surprised when things go wrong! It is vital to understand how your boss likes to operate and what they'd like you to deliver. It also helps to be sensitive to their issues and challenges. If you're very perceptive, you might be able to intuit this, but the safest approach is actually to have the conversation. This should be couched in terms of setting things up to succeed. And it might make sense to talk about what would happen if things go wrong – just so you know what their expectations might be. This does not mean that their answers should necessarily dictate your approach, but if there is a mismatch between what they would ideally like and how you prefer to operate, then you might think about surfacing the differences and exploring whether there is room for compromise.

Be proactive

It is a bit of a cliché these days, but it remains the case that managers prefer to have proactive rather than reactive people working for them – at least, that's what they say. Anticipating events, thinking through how to handle them and then taking action are far better than constantly being caught unawares and having to react to unforeseen circumstances. You should aim to keep your manager in the loop and to share your judgements, not just to ensure that they are not blindsided, but also to demonstrate how proactive you are.

Help them to achieve their business objectives

If the performance management process is working effectively, achieving your own objectives should contribute significantly to your manager achieving theirs. So this is vital for you both. Beyond this, you might think about whether there are areas over and above your own required delivery which would be of benefit to your manager. This might sound somewhat Machiavellian, but remember that your boss's success will reflect well on the team. And if they're the right objectives, and your actions are straight and well intentioned, success will be good for the business overall. It's a classic win–win.

Don't ask questions you could answer yourself

This relates to the classic managerial cry: 'Don't bring me problems, bring me solutions!' And, regardless of whether they articulate it in that way, it's a sentiment that many bosses can relate to. Having a good manager can sometimes be a double-edged sword; you are so in awe of this person, or you crave their approval so badly, that you want to check everything with them. Allied with proactivity is the need to think things through before you go to your boss. Analyse the situation, develop a range of solutions and have a recommendation in mind. You can then use them as a sounding board without coming across as being weak and indecisive. You are also making the best use of time, both the boss's and your own.

Be straight and make your apologies count

Honesty and directness are of critical importance when forging a relationship with your boss, not least when things go wrong. If you do make a mistake, be open about it and, as a priority, work out what you're going to do to rectify the problem – both now and to avoid the same thing happening in the future. Once you have established the solution, it is time to be frank, admit your mistake and make your apology. You need to do this in a strong way and make it clear that you have learned from the experience.

Don't react emotionally

No matter how emotional your boss is themselves, they will not appreciate your being overly emotional. Instead, a calm, rational and considered delivery will be better received – even when you're talking about emotive topics.

Go beyond the call of duty

Proactivity, being solutions orientated and delivering over and above your own objectives all point towards someone who goes beyond the call of duty. That is clear. But there may well be other things you could do. Sharing intelligence, bringing in opportunities, capitalizing on your own network, working extra hours, providing personal insight and just being immensely helpful will all be well received. Just to be clear, though, this is not the same as being sycophantic – sucking up to the boss. It's broader than this; people who really do this well go beyond the call of duty *for the greater good*. They have a real interest in the success of the business, rather than being overly focused on their own profile and perceived performance.

Don't insult your boss's intelligence

Linked with openness and honesty, it is vitally important that you deal with your boss in a straight manner and avoid patronizing them. It goes without saying that you should not tell them lies (though it's remarkable how many people admit that they do). But you'll also need to strike a balance between giving them reasonable reminders of what you've been up to and implying that they have no powers of retention whatsoever. Developing an 'adult to adult' communication style with them – in other words, one which is on a relatively equal footing – is of critical importance.

Ask for and give feedback

Once you've established how your boss likes to work, and you've jointly agreed your objectives, you will need to know how you're getting on. Some people are reluctant to ask for feedback, on the basis that they're nervous about what they'll hear, but everyone needs to know what they're doing well and where there is scope for improvement. It is also valuable to give your boss feedback. Many people in leadership positions complain that it's 'lonely at the top' and that no one tells them anything. Some managers never get any feedback at all, and so it's unsurprising that they continue to do things that are unhelpful or unpopular. A boss needs feedback and – if they're any good – will appreciate the people who give it to them without fear or favour.

Don't get a reputation for being a whinger

Finally, no boss really likes a whinger. Some people are great at what they do, but come in for criticism because they like to have a moan. One IT manager, who was essentially doing two people's jobs, was infamous for her initial response when asked to do anything: she always responded by saying it couldn't be done – and certainly not within the proposed timescales. This criticism came through in her appraisals, but she resisted the feedback on the basis that, in reality, she *always* delivered – and on time. And the evidence supported her assertion. However, others were judging her on her first response. She realized that a deep breath and a more positive reaction was enough to change others' perceptions about her, including her boss, and her subsequent reviews were more positive. So the message is clear: no matter how tempting it is to moan, see if you can keep a lid on it!

What do you do when things go wrong?

What about when it goes wrong? Our research clearly indicated that a poor relationship with a boss is one of the greatest political challenges – and the reason why many people leave the organization they work for. Although the original source is unclear, the observation 'People don't leave companies, they leave bosses' is much cited. Our research certainly supports that; in our qualitative research, most people talked unprompted about problems with their managers – both current and previous.

When things go wrong with the boss, you will be missing out on all of the positive benefits listed at the beginning of this chapter, which a strong line manager can give you. But worse than that, it is one of the greatest sources of workplace stress. It gets in the way of effective working and may be damaging to the team, both in terms of productivity and morale. In extreme instances, you find a department united against a common enemy – the boss! But that's just about the *only* 'positive' knock-on effect that poor management can deliver.

Given that, it's surprising how many individuals are reluctant to stand up to their boss and actively manage the situation. Instead they ask: 'Why should I manage my boss? Surely they're supposed to be managing me?' Or, worse still: 'I'm scared to say anything because it could damage my career.' Avoidance of the conflict and failure to take any responsibility are unproductive. The best that can happen is that the problems continue unchecked. In the worst-case scenario, the situation deteriorates to a level that people just can't tolerate. They then leave.

Consider one thing: your boss may not even know that they are a demotivating manager. We have already talked about how lonely it can be at the top. It's a fact of life that managers, at whatever level, do not get enough feedback from the people who report to them, for the reasons described above. So if your boss is unaware that they are doing anything wrong, what choice do they have but to continue in the same vein? So you have to take action yourself – but it must be the *right* action. What is likely to work in your particular situation?

First, you need to isolate in your mind precisely what it is they do that has such a negative impact. The complaints that people make about their bosses generally fall into four categories. These are given in Table 9.1, along with examples of the extremes that you would expect to find under each heading.

This is by no means an exhaustive list, but it captures the complaints most frequently made about bosses. When it comes to managing the problems they can cause, you have to tailor your approach to your individual circumstance. However, there is an overall pattern which applies in most cases:

1 Define problem.

2 Identify cause.

3 Understand impact.

4 Agree solution.

5 Review.

TABLE 9.1

Flexibility	Attitude
• Flexible vs rigid	• Trustworthy vs untrustworthy
• Listening vs telling	• Ethical vs unethical
• Decisive vs indecisive	• Fair vs unfair
Repression	**Competence**
• Task focused vs people focused	• Organized vs chaotic
• Empowering vs controlling	• Effective vs ineffective
• Developmental vs repressive	• Credible vs lacking respect

In terms of Stages 1, 2 and 3, the guidelines below may help you to clarify your thinking about your particular situation. Stages 4 and 5 are covered at the end of the chapter.

Flexibility

All the issues in this category are concerned with how well your boss strikes a balance between listening to others and taking their ideas on board, and providing direction and leadership. To be managed by a person who is completely inflexible can be frustrating in the extreme, especially if you are someone full of ideas about new ways of doing things. But equally frustrating is a manager who can't make a decision about anything and consults too widely for too long.

Let's first look at the overly controlling boss – the one with too little flexibility. The first step in addressing the situation is to understand why they behave in this way. There might be all sorts of reasons. They may, for instance, be lacking in imagination. Or they're wedded to the past and unwilling to consider any alternative to 'the way we've always done it'. Alternatively, it could be that they are naturally risk averse, cautious, even fearful about change, which can often be accompanied by an inability to trust others. Or they might just be convinced that they're right – every time.

This type of boss inevitably stifles creativity and runs the risk of missing out on opportunities for improvement. A department managed in this way will lag behind others and become known for inflexibility. And it can be quite boring to work there. High flyers will therefore tend to avoid it.

The approach to handling – and ultimately changing – the situation is centred around *confidence building*. You slowly need to gain the trust of your manager and win them over to the notion that new ideas – and other people's ideas – can be useful. But set it up to succeed. You're not likely to get them to say yes unless you build a compelling case, with as much supporting information as possible. The more they see results, and the more they benefit, the more likely they are to be up for innovation and change in the future.

At the other end of the scale, however, you get the boss who is too flexible – they blow with the wind, sit on the fence and lack the courage of their convictions. Our survey indicates that a massive 74 per cent of people complain of decisions being over-turned at a later date. So it's a big problem. Again, you need to understand why they behave in this way. Is it caused by a complete inability to say 'no' up the line? Do their bosses keep moving the goalposts? Are there other factors at play that perhaps you don't know about? Or could it be that the individual has a genuinely open mind – which they are happy to change as new information becomes available? Whatever the cause, this type of leadership too can cause havoc in the shape of errors, rework and duplication. People in the team complain about a lack of direction and inconsistent leadership. Flexibility is one thing, but an unfocused team without an effective leader is quite another.

Dealing with this type of situation is all about *clarifying the brief*. The individual is not going to change overnight. However, you can make sure that the way you manage them minimizes unnecessary work. When you become aware that they are procrastinating, and this is affecting your work, think about what would help them to come to a decision. Could you take it, for instance? And then just let them know what you're doing? If not, is there any extra evidence you could search out and/or provide them with? Or maybe you will need, subtly, to elicit the support of someone else to nudge them in the right direction? And when they do set you a task, make sure you have clearly understood both what is required of you and why. If it's not urgent, delay for a few days and then check back – is it still needed? Give your boss feedback about this tendency to change the requirement and the impact that has. Ask about the underlying reasons and be sympathetic. Monitor the situation and remember to give credit as the situation stabilizes.

Attitude

This often boils down to two main issues:

- the extent to which your boss's attitudes and beliefs coincide with your own, those espoused by the organization, or those held by society as a whole;

- the way in which your boss utilizes formal or positional power; in other words, the power that they have by virtue of their position in the company.

It may not matter that your boss has a different outlook on life from your own – as long as they are not imposing these views on you or refusing to listen to your perspective. However, your boss's influence is considerable and 'pulling rank' is commonplace in organizational life; it's an easy option. You can then find yourself the victim of an abuse of positional power.

In determining how to deal with this problem, two factors are significant:

1 What are their motives?

2 What effect is the problem having on you – and do others share your dissatisfaction?

If you suspect your boss of having negative motives, then you are dealing with a Machiavellian or Barbarian, and all the principles outlined previously in the book apply. For your own protection, it will be wise to be cautious – and to build strong relationships with others elsewhere in the business. You might try to fight fire with fire, by demonstrating Star-like tendencies and developing a strategy to achieve your desired outcome and out-influence them. But do so cautiously.

If, by contrast, you are fairly certain that their motives are sound, it comes down to a simple clash of views, in terms of principles and practice, and you might be successful in attempting a reconciliation.

Which takes us to the second factor: is it just you? If the problem is yours alone – ie the boss doesn't agree with your views – you need to challenge yourself. Is it the case that one of you is right and one of you is wrong, or do both points of view have something to commend them but are in conflict? Your argument will have more chance of prevailing if your boss is out of line with either the organization or society as a whole, or if you can gather together irrefutable evidence to support your position. But if it just comes down to your opinion versus theirs, it's a fact of business life that the boss's view generally carries more weight. This doesn't mean you shouldn't try, however. Chapter 7 on 'Understanding and handling conflict', Chapter 8 on 'Dealing with relationship breakdown' and Chapter 10 on 'Dealing with a bully' go into a great deal of depth on how to address this type of problem.

You are in a stronger position if you find that your colleagues are also dissatisfied. It may be possible to collect feedback from the whole team to validate your own perceptions and – if necessary – to build a case.

In broad terms, dealing with the situation is all about *making your views known*. This needs to be done in a constructive way, pointing out the difference between their view and yours, and the consequent impact. This should not be done in an aggressive way. Think about the encounter in terms of 'problem solving', rather than 'having an argument'. If you have gathered together the views of other people, it's rarely wise to use these as part of your opening gambit. However, if you have tried to be constructive, adopted a problem-solving approach and listened to your boss's point of view, and they *still* fail to listen, you may decide that it will do no harm to reveal that other people share your views. There can be strength in numbers, but there are obvious dangers in being seen as an agitator or the leader of an organized resistance movement.

Above all, it's important to have a real desire to solve the problem. All too often, teams prefer to continue to complain about the boss rather than do anything to address the issues.

Repression

This relates to the extent to which your boss is interested in developing, stretching and 'showcasing' others' talents. It's common sense that the more responsibility you can encourage the team to take, the more productive they will be, and research indicates that they are liable to be more motivated too. So why do so many bosses feel inclined to repress talent and keep people 'in their place'? One answer is that they are insecure in themselves. They are not confident in their own abilities and the way they deal with that is to keep reminding people about how untouchable *they* are in terms of performance – especially since their team is so poor!

Alternatively, it could be that the boss is so extremely task focused that people don't even come into the equation: 'What do you mean, I have to coach and empower my people? I haven't got time to do that – I've got work to do!' This too is surprisingly common. A depressing number of managers still distinguish between the 'people stuff' and the 'day job'.

A third possible cause could be that the individual is risk averse and/or a control freak. This could be driven by a lack of trust in the ability of others and the belief that 'I can do this better than you ever could'.

Whatever the cause of the problem, the result is always the same. Those affected start to stagnate rather than develop or grow. This restricts the impact that the whole team can have and the best people become fed up and leave. In addition, the boss doesn't grow either. They carry on doing the same job month in month out – a job that is probably *at least* one level below what they're being paid to do.

By stark contrast, people who are confident in their own abilities tend to be only too pleased to see the team excelling. They recognize that the success of their people is a credit to their leadership abilities. Instead of clinging on to their Stars, they are delighted to see them promoted out of the team because they are confident that they will become ambassadors elsewhere in the organization.

So how do you persuade your boss to become this empowering, developmental being, if it doesn't come naturally to them? Dealing with the issue is all about *requesting what you're entitled to*. Because many managers do not consider the development of others as a fundamental part of their role, their direct reports too consider personal development to be a luxury. They become nervous about asking for support, guidance and coaching, because they fear it will be seen as wasting their boss's time – and their own. Don't be afraid to ask. Couch your request in terms of how much better you will be able to serve the department, how much greater your productivity will be – in other words, make sure they know what's in it for them. If you suspect that their motivation for suppressing others is a lack of security on their part, emphasize the positive: point out that developing others is a part of their managerial role and will reflect well on them; a strong, well trained team will be a credit to them and a sign of their success. But don't shy away from this one. The more you ask for development, the more you get, the more others follow your lead, and the more your boss will become accustomed to fulfilling this important part of their role.

Competence

Bosses can be inefficient, ineffective and disrespected – unlucky for you if yours is all three! Hopefully you will be able to isolate the problem in just one of these areas. A lack of organization can be due to ignorance – the individual genuinely doesn't know how to organize their time and the workload. But more frequently, it's a question of will. How many people do you know who have been on time management courses but still seem disorganized and panicky? Most people know the theory; it's just a question of putting it into practice. In his book *First Things First*, Stephen Covey talks about the psychopathology known as 'urgency addiction': a complete inability to get excited about anything until the deadline is looming! This is a common phenomenon at all levels of an organization.

Linked with this is the inability to get results – the effectiveness vs ineffectiveness continuum. The reasons for this could be numerous: lack of training, lack of experience, or even lack of confidence. It may also be caused by problems in the other categories, for example, an unwillingness to develop other people, leading to an inability to delegate.

Then there's the issue of credibility – again linked. Clearly, if your boss doesn't get things done – or gets them done, but always late and in a sloppy manner – others will not have respect for them. Alternatively, it could be that your boss does not respect others: a lack of respect for another individual will often provoke the same feeling in return.

Dealing with this type of situation is linked to *giving feedback*. Put yourself in their shoes: if you were in their position, how would you like to receive the feedback? Plan your approach on the basis of that. Your boss can then decide how to deal with the situation. In certain circumstances, it may be appropriate for you to do some upward coaching (see below). Go for it! Coaching doesn't have to follow hierarchical rules.

Agree solution

So you have defined the problem in your own mind, you have considered why your boss might behave in that manner, and you have thought about the impact that their behaviour has – on you, the team and the business. In short, you have prepared your case. But how do you go about agreeing the remedy? There are a number of principles you need to adhere to:

- Pick the right time and place – in private, when you both have the time to dedicate to the issue.
- In your mind, be clear about your desired outcome.
- Be empathic – just because this person is your boss, it doesn't mean to say they don't have feelings too; put yourself in their shoes.
- Give a balanced view – state what you do like about their approach, not just what you don't like.
- Remember at all times that you want to solve the problem.
- Listen to their point of view.
- Be open about the way in which you like to be treated – and explain why.

- Be constructive.

- Offer your suggestions for solutions – don't just present problems.

- Be on the lookout for non-verbal signals, which may indicate that you don't really have their attention or agreement to the fact there's a problem. Examples of this include a failure to make eye contact, an inability to concentrate, general impatience, nodding and agreeing when you don't really feel they're interested, and a lack of listening.

- If appropriate, summarize actions and make sure they agree.

- Work to get their agreement for you – and others – to give them feedback about how well they are doing on an ongoing basis.

Using these principles, it may be appropriate for you to coach your boss. Don't position the meeting as such: it could appear to be presumptuous, patronizing or just plain inappropriate. But you can be in the driving seat – subtly and productively!

Upward coaching

- Set the context: what you are trying to achieve and why.

- Give your feedback: point out what they're doing well first, then, getting things into context, outline the specific constructive criticism and how their behaviour impacts on you and/or the team.

- Ask for their response to that and their perspective on things.

- Agree what needs to change or be achieved. Do not rush this stage. If you don't mutually agree what the problem is and the desired outcome, any further work on planning action will be a waste of time.

- Discuss how things might be changed; don't impose solutions or give your advice without first seeking their views. Listen to them carefully. Build on their ideas and, if appropriate, offer to help – they are, after all, your boss!

- Confirm actions: what needs to be done, by whom and when.

Review

Once you have tackled a particular issue, it is necessary to review the results and maintain the dialogue. Remember that behaviours don't transform themselves overnight, and there are usually hiccups. It is essential to reinforce behaviours that demonstrate your boss is making an effort and also to give feedback when they are slipping back into their old ways. Most people find that it helps to have agreed with their boss that they would give feedback – they then have the licence, the permission to do so.

Once a specific issue seems to be resolved, you are then into a maintenance situation. In other words, there is a need to ensure that the relationship continues to be satisfactory and there's no backsliding – on either part! Bear in mind, however, that people can revert to type, especially under pressure. Don't assume that the backward step represents a trend. But don't be complacent and do nothing either. There are a number of general principles that apply during this maintenance period:

- *Do your bit*: Be helpful, positive and solutions orientated. Don't moan and whinge the whole time – no one likes a daily diet of having their flaws and failings played back to them.

- *Help your boss to do their bit*: Be on their side. Think about what success for them would look like. Tactfully provide them with information.

- *Maintain an open relationship*: Provide them with information and feedback which will help them to achieve their goals – and do it on an 'adult to adult' basis.

- *Learn to say no*: Nine times out of ten your focus should be positive. But you do need to know where to draw the line. If you overload yourself, you run the risk of damaging your overall performance, not to mention your state of mind! So there will be times when you just have to say 'no'. Do it in the right way. Outline all the other tasks you currently have on your plate and ask which of these they are prepared to let slip. Alternatively, suggest someone else who might be able to do the job and offer to brief them.

And when all else fails ...

Finally, there are situations in which, despite having given it your very best shot, you still cannot develop a productive working relationship with your boss, and the conflict continues. The ultimate outcome in this scenario is often that one party or the other leaves – and it's usually not the boss! But before taking such drastic steps, you may think about going to a higher authority. If you have first made every reasonable effort to remedy the situation, and you can state quite clearly what you have done for your part, the senior manager is likely to give you a sympathetic hearing. But be prepared; your immediate boss will inevitably be called in to account for their actions. And once that's happened, they will probably want to have a conversation with you. You need to be prepared for that – both psychologically and organizationally. In advance, work through the following process:

> Preparing an approach:
> - What is the desired outcome in terms of:
>   - your feelings?
>   - your boss's feelings?
>   - the impression you've created?
>   - future working arrangements?
> - How are you most likely to achieve that outcome?
> - What will definitely get in the way?
> - How therefore should you approach the meeting?

Preparing a defence:

- – What are the facts of the current situation?
- – What is the history?
- – What steps have you taken to address the situation?
- – How have those efforts been received by your boss?
- – What caused you to approach your senior manager?

Preparing yourself:

- – Are you happy with the efforts you made to address the situation before you approached the senior manager?
- – If yes: you did everything you felt able to at the time and you were well within your rights to escalate the issue.
- – If no: perhaps you will need to acknowledge you could have done more, but you were still well within your rights.
- – Prepare yourself to take an assertive approach: how can you avoid being aggressive, apologetic or passive?
- – Breathe deeply and try to relax as much as you can.

How you kick off will depend upon the approach your boss decides to adopt. They may well be apologetic and seem determined to solve the situation. However, the safest assumption to make is that this won't happen! It is more likely that they will start the meeting by demanding an explanation from you, in which case you will need to use the defence that you prepared in advance. Outline your views carefully and calmly, all the time trying to maintain eye contact and an assertive approach. You should then ask for your boss's viewpoint on the situation, and listen and respond appropriately. Remember, even if you are initially forced onto the back foot, all is not lost – you can still persist with the more constructive approach that you also prepared in advance. You just need to use your judgement to gauge how useful it would be in the circumstances.

Escalating the matter may feel like an extreme measure, but it can often be what is required to sort the problem out – kill or cure, as they say!

One final thought: remember that your boss is a human being, with their own anxieties and uncertainties. It may be easier than you expect to find common ground.

Chapter Ten
Dealing with a bully

The Manufacturing, Science and Finance Union (MSFU) in the UK has identified workplace bullying as 'persistent, offensive, abusive, intimidating, malicious or insulting behaviour, abuse of power or unfair penal sanctions which make the recipient feel upset, threatened, humiliated, or vulnerable, which undermines their self-confidence and which may cause them to suffer stress'. Peter Randall, author of *Adult Bullying – Perpetrators & Victims*, describes bullying as 'the aggressive behaviour arising from the deliberate intent to cause physical or psychological distress to others'. While in Sweden, where they call it 'mobbing', Klaus Kilmer – who set up a hospital in Sweden to help some of the victims of workplace bullying – coined the phrase 'psychological terrorization'. Clearly, bullying – however you define it – is unacceptable behaviour, which causes pain and distress to those on the receiving end, and undermines their confidence.

So why are we interested in bullying in a book about savvy? Going right back to our initial definitions, being savvy is all about possessing the insight and ability to deal with a wide range of situations in the workplace – and being positively motivated whilst doing so: a Star! Those with negative, suspect motives are Barbarians or Machiavellians, and it is those people who are most likely to demonstrate bullying tendencies – at least, in certain situations and with certain people. They can't see the harm in it: anything to achieve their own ends. Machiavellians tend to be charismatic and plausible, and can get away with unacceptable behaviour for quite some time. By contrast, Barbarians are more obvious to spot and therefore more likely to be caught out. But if they are good at managing up the line, they may escape detection for long enough to inflict significant damage on their victims.

Savvy people recognize bullying, whether they themselves are the victim or they're just witnessing events. They understand how to deal with bullies and make efforts to put an end to such behaviour. And, because of their general approach to working life, they are not usually the chosen prey of a bully – at least, rarely for a second time.

In terms of why it matters, a number of surveys, including our own, have indicated that almost 40 per cent of people have witnessed bullying in the 12 months preceding the research. Women are 50 per cent more likely than men to say that they have witnessed bullying, whilst men are more likely to be described as bullies. Bullying appears to be a greater issue in the public than the private sector, and it seems to be exacerbated in a climate of reforms and cuts. According to Dave Prentis, the general secretary of the Unison union, bullying has doubled in the past decade, a view shared by many employment lawyers. And the result? McAvoy and Murtagh – authors of 'Workplace bullying: the silent epidemic' – say that toxic workplaces have developed as a result of competition, economic rationalism and the current fashion for tough management styles. Cultures like this breed fear, dysfunction and shame amongst colleagues. They cause job-induced stress, depression, anxiety and illness. Over half of the 550 million working days lost annually in the United States are stress related, while the European Agency for Safety and Health at Work estimates that the equivalent figure is 600 million working days across the EU. In the UK alone, at the time of writing, 13.7 million working days are lost every year as a result of stress and depression, while most claims for unfair dismissal and discrimination include some allegation of bullying.

Around two-thirds of people who say they have been bullied attempt to do something about it, but most feel dissatisfied with the outcome. In our recent survey, the majority of people who had experienced bullying themselves ultimately left their organizations; however, with hindsight, most of them concluded that they ought to have engaged more actively and been more effective in challenging the situation.

In the words of one director:

In my last organization, I had a good relationship with the CEO, but he increasingly recruited people he'd worked with before. One key role that he introduced was a person from his old company. The guy in question came in: physically he was quite a big guy and very opinionated. He made it quite clear that he had designs on my area and was looking to be involved in things that frankly were not within his remit. He was not subtle about it. He would go round asking questions and, because he was this big personality, and because of the way he confronted people, he quickly got this reputation for being a bully. People were scared of him and so if he asked for something, they generally complied. So suddenly I'd find he'd taken control of something and we'd all think 'How did that happen?' He and I had quite a few showdowns and it came to a head. He shouted at me and was sarcastic and snide. It became obvious I couldn't win, because, at the end of the day, he'd been recruited by the CEO. This guy was running riot – and not just with me. People were coming to me and complaining. You asked about the outcome? Well, the outcome was that I left.

Being bullied at work can be a traumatic as well as a career-disrupting experience. It's far more common than most people recognize, partly because many victims don't realize that they are being bullied or find it difficult to admit that they are – either to themselves or to others. According to Rayner and Hoelt, there are five categories of bullying behaviour:

1 *Threats to professional status*: where you might be refused promotion or even be at risk of demotion; or be forced to accept a situation which objectively is beneath you; or be removed from important committees or projects; or any other act which diminishes your position or rank.

2 *Threats to personal standing*: linked to professional status, this involves damage to the way in which you are perceived by others – and even yourself; your stock is devalued, your reputation is tarnished and you feel undermined.

3 *Isolation*: where you are cut off from other members of the team, excluded from activities and not kept up to date on developments.

4 *Workload issues*: at one end of the continuum, this can involve being consistently overloaded whilst others are not; at the other extreme, it is where you are never given any interesting projects, you don't have the exposure that others enjoy and you may even be left with very little to do. This can be every bit as stressful as being overworked and has a negative impact on self-esteem, especially where you come in for criticism because of this state of affairs.

5 *Destabilization*: this usually consists of a series of actions and comments, which are designed to undermine confidence, spark self-doubt, cause stress and, in extreme cases, trigger mental illness. A female manager, who had suffered a nervous breakdown many years earlier, was constantly reminded of this by her boss, ostensibly in a caring way. At the same time

as criticizing and isolating the manager, her male boss would frequently comment 'You need to be careful; you don't want to make yourself ill again.' The inevitable happened. She was hospitalized for over six months.

One reason why bullying is so difficult to deal with is that it can have so many different manifestations. Table 10.1 lists bullying behaviours mentioned by people in our survey.

TABLE 10.1

- Nit-picking.
- Fault-finding.
- Undermining.
- Isolating others.
- Excluding others.
- Being hypocritical.
- Being duplicitous.
- Fabricating stories and issues.
- Distorting/twisting the facts.
- Constantly criticizing.
- Abusing disciplinary procedures.
- Imposing verbal or written warnings for trivial reasons.
- Unfair dismissal.

- Singling people out.
- Marginalizing others.
- Belittling others.
- Humiliating others.
- Shouting.
- Threatening.
- Overloading others.
- Underutilizing others.
- Increasing responsibility but removing authority.
- Refusing leave.
- Denying training.
- Imposing unrealistic goals and deadlines.
- Never giving credit for work carried out.

Scan this list and ask yourself: are any of these happening to me, or to any of my colleagues? Where the answer is 'yes', who is responsible? How easy is it to identify the perpetrator – or perpetrators? Do you think their behaviour is deliberate, or could it be the result of a misunderstanding?

All of the behaviours listed can constitute bullying. Tim Field, an expert on the subject, coined the term 'serial bullies': it's not necessarily about you – if you weren't there, they would probably be bullying someone else. The telltale signs of a serial bully are that he or she exhibits a number of the behaviours shown in Table 10.2.

TABLE 10.2

He or She ...

- Is a compulsive liar.
- Has a selective memory.
- Denies everything.
- Is devious, manipulative and spiteful.
- Doesn't listen.
- At times, fails to sustain mature adult conversation.
- Lacks a conscience.
- Shows no remorse.
- Is drawn to power.
- Is ungrateful.
- Is disruptive and divisive.
- Is inflexible and selfish.
- Is insensitive.
- Is insincere.
- Is immature.
- But can also be charming and plausible.

The last point on the list – 'can also be charming and plausible' – is significant. In our consultancy work, we find that the individuals dubbed 'bullies' – usually by the people who work for them – are often perceived by others as charismatic, successful and good to be with. It is this ability to charm that allows the bully to get away with their behaviour for so long. It's also the trait that can give them a big following amongst those who aren't being subjected to the bullying treatment. And it's this attribute which can mean that the victim is initially lured in, with praise, 'trust' and 'helpful' advice, creating a dependency and often a desire to please. At this point, the relationship becomes insidious. The bully withdraws trust and favour. The undermining starts. Their behaviour turns nasty.

Serial bullying tends to follow a pattern, which involves two distinct phases. The first is control and subjugation – the period during which the bully is using some or all of the above behaviours to reduce the victim's self-esteem, self-worth and self-confidence. The second is elimination – removal of the victim from the team or company. Typically, there will then be an interval and then the behaviour will start up again with a different victim.

Cyberbullying

Technological advance does not always bring improvement. Indeed, one factor which has contributed to the doubling in the incidence of workplace bullying over the last decade is the increase in cyberbullying. To date, we have most frequently associated this phenomenon with children and teenagers. However, adults are equally vulnerable to a practice that can take many forms. Offensive e-mails, for instance – even when they are intended as a joke – can be deemed to be cyberbullying, especially when they become a recurring pattern. The effect is, of course, intensified when e-mails and their attachments are copied to many people. One person we talked to, who had complained about being bullied by a co-worker, was regularly shown e-mails criticizing her personally, which the bully had sent to her team. There were also numerous incidents of people finding out they'd been criticized behind their backs on e-mail. The bcc (blind copying) facility can become a vicious weapon in this context.

Alternatively, some people experience e-mails which are overtly threatening. At times, they may appear innocuous – delegating a piece of work, for instance – but the intent of the sender may be more sinister. If the individual is already inundated with work, for instance, and other team members have capacity, then over a period of time even this may constitute cyberbullying.

Then there's the posting of blogs and comments on social networking sites, which can be especially difficult to erase. This becomes much more menacing when it includes personal data, which the victim wouldn't want to be common knowledge. SMS messages too – whether they are threatening, offensive or even suggestive – can be a medium exploited by the cyberbully.

Clearly, many bullies combine face-to-face encounters and electronic media to create a campaign which is traumatic for the recipient. Experienced on a daily basis, the behaviour becomes just too much to cope with.

How to handle a bully

So what should you do when you experience bullying? Here is a five-point plan:

1 Acknowledge the problem.

2 Inform yourself.

3 Confront constructively.

4 Keep a diary.

5 Seek help.

The first step is to *acknowledge the problem* to yourself. Anywhere between 40 and 50 per cent of people (depending on whose research you read) say that they have been bullied during their working life. And many of those responding to the surveys thought that the problem was getting worse, not better.

It's important to resist any temptation to feel shame, embarrassment and guilt. These are normal reactions, but misplaced and inappropriate. They are the sort of feelings that actually help abusers to control and silence their victims. Remember that many people are victims of bullying because they are good at their job and popular with people; the bully is, in fact, jealous or threatened by them. They may have skills and attributes that the bully envies, feels insecure about, and ultimately is determined to undermine.

Another problem can arise as you acknowledge bullying behaviour: the actions involved may be so subtle, and the bully so plausible, that when you talk about what they're doing, other people may try to excuse their behaviour with the result that you come to wonder whether perhaps you're just overreacting. To quote one victim from our survey: 'She always criticized, and never praised – ever! And she always blamed others. She even managed to pin two problems on me when I was on holiday. But when I talked to other people about it, my issues with her just sounded stupid. I thought it had to be me.' And then there's the problem of vicious cycles, which can increase self-doubt. This same individual went on to say: 'The trouble was that whenever I saw her, I became anxious, anticipating her criticism. The anxiety then actually caused me to make more mistakes. Which, of course, meant that I would come in for more criticism. I felt as though I wasn't doing a good job any more.' This is exactly what the bully wants. So it is important to remain objective and assertive. Stand by your judgement: don't let a bully wriggle off the hook. And don't make yourself into a victim.

The second step is to *inform yourself*. Read up on the subject. The problem of bullying has burgeoned, as evidenced by the number of employment tribunals. Which at least means that there is a lot of information available to those who feel as though they might be being victimized. Take a look at the websites. Employment lawyers say that many tribunals can be avoided if victims are prepared to take action. It may be sufficient to *confront constructively*: point out to the individual what they are doing and the impact it is having. In a number of cases, the individual accused will be concerned – even horrified – by the way they are perceived; the behaviour was unconscious and the consequences unintended. They may feel moved to take immediate action to address the situation, if it genuinely was a misunderstanding or misjudgement. However, this is unlikely to be the case when the person you are dealing with is a serial bully.

You will need information to support your case. It is important to *keep a diary* of any instances of abuse or mistreatment, to save copies of relevant e-mails and other documentation, and to gather other evidence. One of the participants in our research compiled such a dossier, including the CCTV footage which proved that she did not take the two-hour lunch she was accused of taking (one in a litany of complaints), but that she had been only three minutes late. This was an individual who rarely took a break! From a legal perspective, a one-off incident is seldom considered as bullying: you need to establish a barrage of snide and sarcastic remarks, and/or the constant drip-feeding of unfounded allegations, and/or the ongoing undermining of your authority and confidence. You must make sure that you have captured the *series* of events if your case is to hold water.

Equally, if you have been accused or criticized unfairly, put in writing a request for the bully to expand upon the allegation. It needs to be phrased carefully and as unemotionally as possible. Ask a trusted friend or colleague to look through it for you with a critical eye, testing for anything that could be perceived to be provocative or inflammatory. If the bully doesn't reply to your initial request, put it in writing again, commenting that you haven't received a response to your initial communication.

So you have put together your case, but who can you turn to? You need someone from whom you can *seek help*. Ideally you would approach your line manager to explain what has been going on and the impact it has had – both on you and on the team. But what if the bully involved *is* your line manager? If you have already tried to challenge them and the situation does not improve, you will need to try a different tack. Perhaps one of the following:

- Talk to your Personnel or HR department for advice.

- Most organizations these days have policies and guidelines to deal with such problems. Ask for a copy of your employer's bullying and harassment policy. You might wish to do this discreetly (eg through a third party) if you're not yet ready to challenge the bully.

- Find out about the official grievance procedure and follow it.

- Many unions are aware of the existence and impact of bullying at work – and are sympathetic to those being subjected to it. You may therefore consider talking to your union representative.

- Contact one or more of the many helplines that have been set up to deal with just this issue.

- If your physical or psychological health has suffered, contact your GP or your occupational health unit at work.

- Get in touch with a lawyer.

It is completely understandable, however, that if you have been subjected to bullying, you may not feel strong enough, brave enough or – somewhat surprisingly – sufficiently embittered to take any of these courses of action. You may think they are too drastic or you may not want to 'go public' on what is happening, preferring instead to try to tackle the issue yourself. If so, the first thing to do is to examine whether you are doing anything that makes you more likely to be a victim. Are there any victim-like words, phrases and behaviours that you use? What do you do or say that might make you fair game for the office bully? Do you find yourself saying any of the following?

- 'Mustn't complain.'
- 'I'm sure they didn't mean any harm.'
- 'I'm probably imagining it.'
- 'They've no doubt got their own problems.'

- 'What else can you expect?'
- 'It's probably my own fault.'
- 'I suppose I ought to …'
- 'I don't like to cause a fuss.'

Apologizing too much (even when it's clearly not your fault), always assuming the blame, a tendency towards feelings of guilt and being too tolerant are all factors which may make you look like a soft target to a bully looking for their next victim. Other indicators of vulnerability include: a lack of assertiveness (although you may behave aggressively), a tendency to worry too much about what other people think of you, and general naivety. In our research, those people who self-score as naive are almost 50 per cent more likely to say that they have witnessed bullying than those in other categories. Furthermore, when the bully is someone who is popular with others, a desire to be liked can make it incredibly difficult for the victim to stand up to them or take action to redress the situation.

Recognizing that you may be doing things to make the situation worse can be as significant a step forward as acknowledging that you are being bullied. Listen to yourself, then make a real effort to abolish any phrases which suggest you'll always take the blame or that you'll put up with anything. Become more assertive in your approach (there are a lot of good training courses aimed at helping you develop in this area). Convince yourself that things can change: you don't any longer have to put up with what you have accepted in the past.

And as a manager … ?

The ethos within your team is critical. Teams that enjoy a constructive, harmonious and collaborative culture are less likely to experience – or tolerate – bullying behaviour. Conflict, when it arises, should be healthy and creative. When it's not (because, of course, there will always be arguments), the disagreement should be dealt with promptly and in a constructive, fair manner. Issues which are left to fester tend to become exaggerated – blown out of all proportion. Innocent bystanders get involved and collude merely by listening to complaints, by observing the unacceptable behaviours and by doing nothing to remedy the situation.

Teams which promote 'healthy competition' may find that the competitive spirit is taken too far. This can lead to negative politicking – for instance, back-stabbing, blaming others or rubbishing their contribution – which, if not nipped in the bud, can rapidly turn into bullying. If, as a manager, you tend to subscribe to the 'divide and rule' leadership style, you run the risk of encouraging unhealthy competition and breeding suspicion amongst team members. You may even be laying yourself open to charges of bullying. So be aware of this: are you taking it too far?

As far as individuals are concerned, it is vital to be alert to the well-being of every person who works for you. Look for signs of negative stress. Be vigilant. If there is any tailing off in performance, or motivation, try to find out the causes. Encourage people to talk. Listen and empathize. Take the situation seriously. Ask 'How are things at work?' – and ask it regularly. Also, attend to individuals' personal development. Coaching and other forms of training can help people to build their assertiveness and confidence, as well as their powers of persuasion, moving them more into the Star camp and reducing the risk that they will fall prey to bullying.

Throughout this chapter, we have acknowledged that being bullied can be a traumatic experience. We have also reported that many participants in our survey believe that bullying is on the increase, as a consequence of the anxieties and pressures associated with a difficult economic climate. Tough times may be leading people in some companies to behave more selfishly and ruthlessly, in the belief that personal survival can only be achieved at the expense of colleagues. However, there are also some grounds for optimism. In other companies, the culture seems to be promoting a different response – an attitude closer to 'United we stand, divided we fall' rather than 'Dog eat dog' and 'Devil take the hindmost'! Corporacy and collegiacy become the watchwords, with management based on reaching informed consensus rather than command and control. The latter is, of course, the management style most tolerant of bullying. And the shift away from it goes hand in hand with the tightening of employment legislation designed to eliminate bullying.

Chapter Eleven
Making networks work for you

It's not what you know, but who you know!

In our survey, over two-thirds of respondents agree with this statement. Unusually, this is one area in which men and women are in accord; there is no difference of opinion. However, if you work in the private sector, you are much more likely to agree than if you are in the public sector. Critically, according to our definition, the more savvy you consider yourself to be, the more likely you are to appreciate the need for networking.

It's probably fair to say that networking has always been of the utmost importance in achieving business success. For many people, friends and family were instrumental in helping them get their first job. Others have kind – and well connected – contacts to thank for new business wins. And strings have always been pulled to get children into schools or, later on, into universities. Nepotism and 'the old school tie' are more frowned upon as we strive for a fairer, more meritocratic society, but it would be naive to suggest that they are no longer powerful influences.

This was borne out in our research interviews; at some point in the conversation – unprompted – every interviewee brought up networking as a critical component of savvy. Here are a few quotes:

'My boss is savvy. He gathers a lot of information, probably by giving away a little. He knows who's important and understands the informal hierarchy. This has been an education for me. It's not just about knowing lots of people. More about understanding who, in that network, will be more influential when you need to get something done.'

'Building relationships is key to savvy. You don't need to like everybody, but you should have a healthy respect. Treat people in the way you would like to be treated yourself.'

'Savvy is someone who knows how the organization works ... they have a network of contacts in different departments and organizations and if they don't know where to start or need to find something out, they can ring one of those friends. This can often save weeks!'

So what's changed? Do you need to feel doomed if you didn't go to the 'right' university? Or destined for a mediocre career if your family doesn't enjoy the right connections? Networking, though still critical, has changed. According to our research:

- Networking has become more professional and above board. In the most recent annual appraisal process of one large financial services company around two-thirds of all people had a development need identified for them, which related to the need to improve networking skills.

- Networks have opened up – no longer do you have to go to the 'best' schools or belong to the 'best' families. People are more frequently rewarded on merit. You do, however, still need to be good at networking!

- More people, in a wider variety of different jobs, now accept that they must develop their networking skills. Why? Not least, because there is greater mobility and uncertainty in the job market. But also because we are expected to be more entrepreneurial, opportunistic and solutions orientated now than previously.

Whilst men and women agree how important networking is in being successful at work, there is a difference in how comfortable they feel doing it. It is not that women lack the skills required to be effective networkers, more a question of their attitude towards the desirability of networking. Furthermore, they perceive that men are conditioned to network from an early age. When you dig deeper, women are more inclined to admit to the feeling that they shouldn't *have* to resort to networking: they would rather allow their performance to speak for itself rather than – as they see it – 'have to blow their own trumpets'. They are also more likely to feel they don't have time. In over a decade of work with women focused on developing networking abilities, I have found that it is far more important for them to change their attitude than to acquire any new skills. For this reason, we will cover mindset later in the chapter.

What are networks?

Networks are merely groups of acquaintances – people you know or know of. At the most informal end of the scale, they are individuals you might pass the time of day with, bump into at the company social club, see at a parents' evening, or whatever. As networks become more formal, there tends to be some common interest or agenda. Certainly, colleagues you collaborate with elsewhere in the business fall into this category. But it might be outside work, a sporting connection, for example, or a club – in fact, anything you're a member of or a participant in.

If you ask people to draw their personal network, most come up with a *hub* diagram. They place themselves at the centre – the hub – with their connections arranged around them. This, however, is a pretty primitive way of viewing a network. What about the people our contacts know, that we don't? Who might we be connected to indirectly? We need to think on a broader basis than we have done in the past.

Why network?

We have established that networking is perceived to be important, particularly if you want to be successful in business; but why? What is the purpose of networking? There are five basic types of network:

1 social;

2 information;

3 interest;

4 profile;

5 opportunity.

The *social* network is just as it sounds – individuals with whom you socialize or have done so with in the past. It contains all the friends and acquaintances that exist in your private life, ranging from people you've known since you were a child to recent 'acquisitions'. They may be dear friends you see all the time, or contacts you've never met but keep up with on Facebook. Some people are rigorous about drawing the line between personal and professional – and never the twain shall meet. Others are constantly on the lookout for opportunities to migrate people from the social network to one of the other categories.

The *information* network is all about keeping up to date with what's going on. You can tap into the latest thinking or find someone to act as a sounding board for your own ideas. Membership of this type of network gives you a broader perspective and can provide you with a wealth of information, which makes you a useful person to know back in the workplace. As well as face-to-face contact, this particular type of network is great for social networking sites, Twitter, etc. People from your information network can easily migrate into the three remaining types of network – and often in a mutually beneficial way – so it's important to be alert to this potential.

The *interest* network aims to do something more than merely share facts and ideas amongst its membership. Of course, information will be a key element, but members of this type of network are focused on achieving common goals. These may be general aims and aspirations, like a professional body working to advance the industry and maintain standards. Or they may have very specific objectives. For instance, in recent years, many financial and professional services firms have set themselves targets for increasing the percentage of women at more senior levels. As part of this drive, many firms have established a dedicated network of colleagues which, amongst other things, will provide development and opportunities for women.

Profile networks tend to be personal – being seen in the right places, making contact with the right people, and so on. But they could equally be about enhancing the status of a team or project. Some people find this type of profile-raising activity to be embarrassing – even slightly shameful. But it's a fact of life that senior managers have an enormous number of direct and indirect reports. As a consequence, they may remember only a few – and are likely to credit those who are uppermost in their minds with the successes. It is the people who volunteer for projects, approach work proactively, make things happen and sing about their successes who are more memorable. The results are obvious. It is also important to build profile beyond the organization in which you currently work, particularly during periods of uncertainty. The upsurge in sites like LinkedIn, the business-related social networking site, is testament to the importance of being connected externally.

Finally, *opportunity* networks are the mainstay of business success. They involve establishing clearly what you want for the future – short, medium and long term – and identifying people who will be able to assist you in achieving your aspirations. Few senior positions are filled by respondents to newspaper advertisements. Most go to existing contacts, some of which may have been made relatively recently. And cold calling is less effective when developing new business than a recommendation from someone in your network. It really is who you know that will make a difference to your business effectiveness. During the global financial crisis towards the end of the last decade, levels of opportunity networking soared exponentially – for obvious reasons. Those who were approached reported that they received so many requests for coffees and meetings that they tended to respond positively only where they felt a connection. Individuals who'd ignored them for months or, worse still, had treated them badly in some way, were rarely accommodated, demonstrating quite clearly that you need to lay the foundations for productive opportunity networks early on – and avoid making enemies!

Are you a natural?

So how easily does it come to you? Are you one of those people who always seems to 'know a man who can'? Or are you merely someone who observes this type of behaviour – somewhat enviously – wondering where on earth they've managed to conjure that contact up from? Like many things in life, some people are naturals, and others aren't. Answer the questions in Table 11.1 to find out if networking comes naturally to you. Score yourself 2 if the statement completely describes you, 1 if it somewhat describes you, and 0 if it's not you at all.

TABLE 11.1

	Score		Score		Score
1. I am quick to pick up the phone.		2. I feel very stimulated by anything new.		3. I like to work things out for myself.	
4. I get bored rather easily.		5. I always read about who's doing what in the newspaper.		6. I prefer to write to people than phone them.	
7. I'm not scared to ask for support from people.		8. I'm always introducing people to each other.		9. My daily contact with people is limited to a few close colleagues.	
10. I quickly take advantage of new opportunities.		11. At parties, I'm always fascinated to hear about what others do.		12. I feel uncomfortable asking for favours.	
13. I'm always on the lookout for new ideas.		14. I really enjoy getting out and about.		15. I would describe myself as an introvert.	
16. I know how to use social networking sites.		17. I'm always happy to ask for an introduction to someone.		18. I don't see why I should have to network.	
Column 1 total		**Column 2 total**		**Column 3 total**	

Add the total scores of columns 1 and 2, then subtract the total of column 3. The maximum score is 24 and if you are anywhere near this mark you are a true networker. In fact, any score of over 16 is pretty good. A total of 8 to 16 is OK, but you should examine any statement, in columns 1 or 2, for which you scored zero, along with any score of 2 in column 3, and think about the implications. A total of less than 8 suggests that networking is really not up your street at all. However, even those who score negatively can make progress in this area – provided they want to, and as long as they do it in a way which is consistent with their personality and values.

What are the skills and behaviours?

So if you want to enhance your ability to network effectively, what are the skills and behaviours you require?

Clearly, networking is all about people. So you need up-to-date knowledge of who's who. It helps to take a genuine interest in others, which most people don't have a moral, conceptual issue with, but for some it takes some effort to develop this concern. Asking around, reading about who's doing what, trying to identify who knows whom all help. The ultimate aim, of course, is to identify where the power lies which, to some, will sound Machiavellian. However, this cannot be the case if your motives are altruistic. It's simply about having influence.

Linked to this, it is important to be curious about corporate changes and strategic direction. What's important for the business, how does this affect you and how, therefore, can you contribute? Demonstrating proactivity is a critical factor in effective networking.

It might also help to remember that being communicated with is not a God-given right! In many organizations, it may be necessary to go and find out what's going on rather than complaining that no one tells you anything. Asking questions, listening carefully to what people are saying and reacting appropriately are all crucial components of effective communication and relationship building. Other dimensions include being assertive (but not aggressive), knowing what you want and being self-confident. To make sure you don't overdo it, you might ask yourself whether your request feels reasonable, whether it's good for the business and whether you feel comfortable asking. If it's just the last of the three which is giving you a problem, you may need to consider the implications of the section on mindset later in this chapter.

Who's in your network?

Ten years ago, when we asked people to map their networks, they would generally draw the whole thing – all of their contacts on one piece of paper, albeit a large one! This would barely be possible today – we know so many people. So the first thing to do is to clarify your specific goal. Do you wish to raise your profile generally or are you trying to work out what your next career move should be? Is the aim to generate revenue for the business or do you want to benchmark yourself against competitors? The list of objectives that can be achieved through networking is endless. So be clear what exactly the desired endgame is. Of course, you may have multiple goals, some of which are inextricably linked. This is fine; just so long as you have clarity about what you're trying to accomplish.

Then identify who will be able to help you. Draw yourself in the middle of a large sheet of paper and start to build up a picture of your own network as it relates to this specific object. Place the people with whom you have a strong working or personal relationship close to you in the centre, and those who are less known to you further out. Use the size of the circle to indicate how important that particular contact will be in terms of helping you achieve your goal. Include within the diagram those people who are external to your organization, as well as those within it. Once you have done this, join yourself to each of the contacts. Along these adjoining lines, write what you want from them, the nature of the connection and the influence they have over you. Then add what you might be able to offer them. Be imaginative and don't let false modesty get in the way of good analysis. Finally, add in any relationships that they have with each other but you are not involved with. See Figure 11.1 for an example.

FIGURE 11.1   Networking objective: change in career

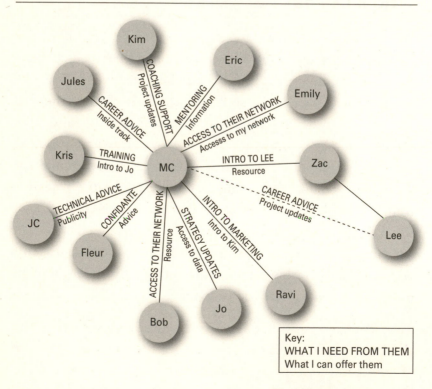

Review the whole picture. Do you know the right people – or have contacts who can introduce you to the right people? Where do they all sit? What is the ratio of internal to external? Is the balance appropriate, given your objective? Once you have mapped out all the key relationships, it might make sense to segment, or group, your audience. For instance, who are the really important people? Of these, who will you find it easy to make contact with? They could be your priority targets. Then you will need to focus on those who are important, but who you don't find so easy or who you're more remote from. How can you best build a relationship with these people? What do you know of them? What are they like? What do you think they might want from you? And, given all that, how can you best influence them? From this analysis, you might wish to draw up a plan, factoring in the priorities. And don't forget that, whilst you've been concentrating on focused objectives, when you actually do your networking, there might be other spin-off benefits. For example, in Figure 11.1, you might want to talk to Zac about introducing you to Lee, and in return you are going to offer Zac resource of some kind, but you might also take the opportunity to pick his brains about another matter, which will provide invaluable information for you and will leave Zac feeling pleased to have been consulted.

Who *might* be in your network?

Ross Gittel and Avis Vidal coined the phrases 'bonding' and 'bridging' to describe two different types of networking. Most of the networking we do is known as 'bonding'. This involves forming and maintaining relationships between homogeneous groups of people. And all of us – whether we're alert to it or not

– are part of a number of discrete networks. Over and above this, sophisticated networkers are alert to 'bridging' opportunities, which is all about building connections between homogeneous groups. So, for example, the head of a practice group in one firm has an internal network. So too does his counterpart in a competitor firm. When they are introduced to one another by a third party who knows them both, this is bridging. And why would they want to meet? Perhaps to benchmark their offerings. Or to think about new possibilities in the market. There are a whole host of reasons why competitors might want to get together. However, the savvy networker always considers potential downsides, and squares the encounter with people who might wonder what on earth they're up to, reassuring them that they're not looking for another job, or selling the firm's secrets! The same applies to contacting someone else's client, talking to a senior manager in another department and so on. We all need to bond – this is part and parcel of everyday life – but, if we want to get ahead, we need to find opportunities for bridging.

The savvy networker is also alert to 'structural holes', which are merely gaps in networks. They then create bridges to span these holes, fulfilling a 'broker' role.

How to do it – the mindset

If you feel uncomfortable with the prospect of networking, either generally or with regard to one specific interaction, this is likely to come across loud and clear. If this is a problem for you, here are three tactics you can employ to put you in the right frame of mindset and help you convey the right impression:

● Visualize how you want to come across.

● Put yourself in their shoes.

● Reframe your thinking.

Visualizing how you want to come across merely involves establishing what impression you want to make – how would you like the other person to perceive you? What do you want them to say about you afterwards? List the adjectives you'd like them to use when describing you, then think through what you could do to convey that impression. Close your eyes and imagine that you are behaving in this manner. Assume success. Feel confident in the interaction. Strange as it might seem, research clearly indicates that if you are able to summon up a robust and rounded vision of yourself engaging in a particular activity, then you are more likely to behave that way. The technical way to describe this effect is that your 'inner programmes' have taken over.

As far as putting yourself into their shoes is concerned, it is staggering how many people feel at a disadvantage when networking. They might consider the other person to be too busy, too remote or too grand to be interested in what they have to say, leading to feelings of 'I'm just wasting their time' or 'It's too much trouble for them'. This is not constructive. Nor is it usually true; if you have mapped out your network properly, you will have given consideration to 'what's in it for them'. So it is important to be positive about the contact and to think about it in terms of being mutually beneficial. When was the last time that someone asked you for help or advice? How did you feel about it? Flattered? Only too pleased to help? Bear in mind that most other people feel the same way.

Finally, reframe your thinking. We introduced the concept of reframing in Chapter 2 and have referred to it since. It merely involves being in tune with your thoughts, recognizing when they are negative or unconstructive, and then turning them around – ideally by 180° – to put you in a positive frame of mind. To help you, Table 11.2 gives some examples that are specific to networking.

TABLE 11.2

Negative, unconstructive thought	Positive, reframed thought
They don't have time for this.	Of course they have time; that's why they're seeing me.
I feel much too junior.	We are adults and colleagues. Therefore we're equal.
I am embarrassed to ask for this favour.	I am perfectly entitled to ask (besides, it's in the company's interests).
They intimidate me.	I am perfectly capable of dealing with this person – and I'm well prepared.
Supposing they say no ...	They probably won't, but if they do that's fine too – at least I will have asked.
What if others see me as a sycophant – or if the person I'm addressing is?	I'm comfortable with my motives and I don't care what others might think.

Finally, if it's at all possible, try not to pin all your hopes on one contact. If you have other irons in the fire, there is less danger of you sounding desperate! Remember you're not asking for a job or begging for business. Instead, you are conducting research, looking for advice or seeking contacts. Most business people do it – and know it's the basis of success.

How to do it – the meeting

Having ensured that you are in a positive frame of mind, it's critical to get the meeting right. The point was alluded to above, but it's so vitally important that it is repeated here: have a very clear idea of what it is you want to achieve and, if at all possible, think about what you might offer in return. If you've done your research, you will have some idea about their personality and therefore what they are most likely to respond to. What are the hooks? You may well need to be creative in your approach and think laterally.

Timing is also key. Make sure you act well in advance. The development of a good business relationship takes time. Ideally, you would start gently and develop mutual trust, respect and interest. And even if it's a small favour or piece of advice you're after, people will not thank you for putting pressure on them at the last minute.

Duration too is important. Many busy people have their calendars mapped out in 30-minute slots – and their days are filled with meetings. So you're more likely to get agreement to half an hour than an hour.

How are you going to position the meeting? Most people make contact first by e-mail, so – having agreed to see you – the other individual will have some inkling of what you want to talk about. But don't assume they have remembered; your opening statements need to be clear and concise. And checking what *they* want to get out of the meeting will help to ensure that you are on an equal footing – it's not just a favour for you.

As well as the introduction, you should also think through the questions you definitely want to ask. Be aware, however, that two basic questions, combined with active listening and intelligent responses to what they say, can easily fill half an hour – or longer! By all means have a checklist of what you'd like to ask: it'll be invaluable if your contact turns out not to be very communicative. But be clear about which are the essential questions, and which the 'nice to haves'. One question that is always useful to ask is whether they know of any other people who would be able to help you out.

FIGURE 11.2

- Avoid being overly deferential

- Establish your objectives for
  the meeting

- Focus on your business

- Talk (aim for a maximum
  50% of the airtime yourself)

- Avoid being arrogant

- Establish what they want to
  get out of the meeting

- Focus on their business

- Listen (though some people will
  need to be persuaded to open
  up)

And when you're face to face with them, develop rapport, make eye contact and read their body language. These are all important factors when it comes to leaving a good impression.

Successful meetings – and the start of strong business relationships – often require a series of balancing acts on your part. See Figure 11.2.

As you go through the meeting, you might think about how well you're striking these balances. Are you nervously talking too much? Or not saying enough? Are you wringing your hands obsequiously? Or cockily failing to demonstrate any respect at all for the other person? 'Chunking up' is a technique that many savvy networkers use. This involves moving the debate to a higher level in an attempt to identify common ground. Questions like 'What is this a part of?' or 'What is this symptomatic of?' or 'How does this tie in with the strategy?' all help to move the debate to a higher level.

Of course, as you get to the end of the meeting, it helps to 'chunk down', which involves talking about specific follow-up and next steps – moving more into the detail.

Make sure you manage the time. Do not use up more time than you've requested. Not, that is, unless *they* seem intent on continuing the debate. Nor should you leave them with actions. It's your project. You should be responsible for the follow-up activity.

After the meeting, write and thank your contact, where appropriate summarizing what happens next. This is a matter of courtesy and it makes them more inclined to help you out in the future. Perhaps they'd think of introducing you to others. A written reminder certainly means you stay in their minds for longer.

How to do it – the event

Many people fear networking events. In the words of one senior woman who goes to cocktail parties two or three times a week, 'I absolutely dread it. I don't like strangers. I hate walking into a room where I don't know anyone.' She then went on to say, 'But I do it. And people say that I'm good at it.' The issue is not her capability or her performance, it's the way she feels about it. When approaching an event, therefore, it is critical to have the right mindset. Reframing, as described above, will help.

And you need to be certain why you're doing it. Do you want to make contacts, secure a meeting, raise your profile or just enjoy yourself? Clearly, from a business perspective, the last point may not be the most lucrative objective, but at times it is perfectly legitimate. For instance, at a leaving party, the guests might just want to have a fun time. They don't want to be sold to. But to make the event worthwhile from a professional viewpoint, you might wish to leave others with the feeling that they'd really like to see you again. Being clear about your goal(s) will help you to determine your strategy.

Preparation is key. Do you know who is likely to be there? If so, which people do you want to meet? For each, you will need to think through a) what you want to achieve and b) how you might approach them. Of course, there is a possibility that you don't need to put your plan into action; you might get lucky and someone else introduces you. But to have a plausible reason for talking to them will help in the absence of serendipity.

You might also benefit from developing the skill of drawing others into a conversation. This serves two purposes:

- It includes other people, who might otherwise feel excluded and awkward.

- It reduces the risk that you are caught in a one-to-one conversation that you feel uncomfortable about moving on from.

On that subject, are you clear about how you could move on if the situation demands it? Whilst to some this could sound 'mean', you are there for a reason and to fulfil your objectives completely, you need to get to all the people you planned to meet. This means that it would be counterproductive to spend your entire time with a single person – unless, of course, you find that this one conversation surpasses all your expectations and provides a rich vein of opportunity. Let's be realistic, people expect you to move on! And you might be doing them a favour by doing so. It should be quite simple to say 'It's been great talking to you, but you must excuse me, because I promised to catch up with someone,' although some people find it immensely difficult, because they feel it might appear rude. It's not!

So, attempt to be relaxed and not try too hard. Be authentic, not someone you're not. Remember your objectives. And try to make the event worthwhile for you.

After the event comes the most crucial element: follow-up. Some people like to log the actions as soon as they leave, so that they don't forget anything or anyone. And then be true to your word. If you've said you'll send an interesting paper to someone, send it! If you have promised to have coffee, get it fixed in the diary, even if it's six weeks away. Conscientiously go through your actions, remembering that the follow-up should also be structured and planned. If you're having lunch, what do you want to achieve then? How would you advance this relationship or opportunity? Networking is not rocket science but it is a skill – and one that requires discipline and energy.

How to do it – social networking sites

At the time of writing, Facebook has over 750 million active users. Users develop profiles with pictures, lists of interests, contact information and other personal information. They can create 'updates' which will appear in a central news feed for friends to see. But it's not just a personal tool. As well as personal profiles for individuals, businesses may also develop a free page that can be used to promote their products and services. This can allow them to give a description of what their business does, create a portfolio and invite people to events. Users can ask friends or other businesses to 'like' a page and from there, hope that friends of friends may choose to 'like' their page. Business pages are normally open to any Facebook user to 'like' and can be found by using the search option.

As with personal Facebook account users, a business may update its status and upload images, which will appear on the news feed of anyone who has chosen to 'like' the business. This can be used as a marketing tool for current special offers or simply to raise awareness of the business and achieve more 'likes'. Facebook provides businesses with a tool to see how many people 'like' them and how many people look at updates. This tool is known as 'insights' and will help the business to realize which status updates have been more successful with regards to interactions.

As a business page user, the key to updating your status on Facebook is to keep it interesting to as many people as possible and to get the right balance as to how often this is done. The acceptable frequency is probably between once a week to a couple of times a day, depending on your specific needs. Any more often than this and you may be accused of spamming. Any less frequently and people may forget about who you are. Either way, this could lead to people 'unliking' you and being lost by you as a potential contact forever.

CASE STUDY

I decided to create a business page on Facebook in 2009 when it seemed like it was becoming a popular marketing tool. I had the attitude that I would give it a try – it was free, after all! Big businesses can have thousands of people who 'like' them. My business page currently has just over 100 'likes'! I still have a way to go! Having said this, I have gained many new contacts through friends recommending me to friends and businesses on Facebook. This has led to new work so I think it has been worthwhile so far!

LinkedIn has been set up purely for professional purposes. There are approximately 120 million users worldwide and it is one of the fastest growing social networking sites, with 69 of the Fortune 100 companies using it.

Users create a profile that outlines all their credentials, including employment history, and recommendations from other users. This includes a list of contact details of people with whom they have some level of relationship, called 'connections'; anyone (whether a site user or not) can become a connection. A contact network is built up consisting of their direct connections, the connections of each of their connections (termed second-degree connections) and also the connections of second-degree connections (termed third-degree connections). This can be used to gain an introduction to someone a person wishes to know through a mutual contact.

Employers can list job openings that they would like to fill and view potential candidates' profiles. People seeking work can follow different companies that they would be interested in working for and review hiring managers' profiles to see which of their existing connections could introduce them. Job seekers can research the companies that they wish to apply to and see statistics about the companies such as how many people they employ, different job titles and ratios of women to men. Applicants can now use a 'Apply with LinkedIn' feature on the site using their resumes on their profile to apply to a job.

In terms of how you can make LinkedIn work for you, the following guidelines should be helpful:

- Remember it's all about you. What is your brand and how can you differentiate yourself from other users? See Chapter 12 for some thoughts on that.

- Develop a marketing strategy. What are you trying to achieve? Who, therefore, are you trying to reach and what information do you need to share?

- Try to reach second- and third-degree connections. The wider you spread your network, the more likely you are to identify and capitalize on opportunities.

- Join Groups. This also has the effect of creating more opportunities.

- Be visible and helpful – store up credit. You want to become known as a useful connection and others are more likely to help you out if you've done something for them in the past.

- Ask people to recommend you.
- Keep your profile up to date, relevant and complete.

There are, of course, other social networking sites, most of which can be used to enhance your professional standing and status, and expand your business network. Whilst they are not mentioned here, many of the same rules apply. You need to be focused and active. You need to reach out. You need to do things for other people. And you need to ask for favours and recommendations in return.

Good people to know

'The success of any kind of social epidemic is heavily dependent on the involvement of people with a particular and rare set of social gifts. It is the idea that in any situation roughly 80 per cent of the 'work' will be done by 20 per cent of the participants' (Malcolm Gladwell, *The Tipping Point*).

Given that, it is vital to know who best to hook up with. Who are the people worth knowing, the people who are delivering 80 per cent of the overall contribution? Gladwell talks about a range of roles, generally fulfilled by different individuals, all of which are immensely useful. Firstly, you have the *connectors* – the brokers referred to above – who link us up with the world. They are the classic networkers. They are informed and interconnected. They know where the power lies. They understand when it's worth getting people together. And they have an extraordinary ability to build relationships with others.

Different, but equally useful, are the *mavens*. These are information specialists, who are also, as Gladwell puts it, almost pathologically helpful. They don't just accumulate information about the marketplace, they also want to share it – and to help others solve their problems. In this way, they contribute to the social epidemic.

And the third role that Gladwell identifies is that of the *salesman*, which is exactly as it sounds. These charismatic people possess immense powers of persuasion and strong negotiation skills. They are adept at getting others to say yes to them and, importantly, to want to say yes.

Think about your own network map. Can you identify any of these characters? If so, how can you build relationships with them that both further your own objectives and are also mutually beneficial? Think of yourself too. If you were to be known as one of these three, what would it be? Are your talents aligned with a maven-style role? Or are you more of a salesman or connector? Having some sense of where your potential lies – and also where your interests are – will help you to become the right kind of networker for you.

Maintaining your network

Your network will develop and mature over time. People will drop out, others will fill their shoes. And as your career progresses, the number, range and depth of your relationships with others will grow. But your database of contacts is like a garden: without care and maintenance, the whole thing becomes tangled and unwieldy. At that stage, the only thing you can do with it is prune heavily and pretty much start again. Consequently, you need to manage and maintain your network. This means finding a way of being in regular contact with people. And regular means appropriate! For some people, an occasional e-mail will suffice – enough to show that you are still interested in them. With others, you may need to see them on a regular basis to demonstrate your support. Listen carefully to what they have to say and make a note of any developments in their lives. Try to understand what matters to them. In these days of technological dominance, some people have said that they feel quite moved by a handwritten note – it's so much more effort! Others, however, might consider it anachronistic.

Above all, be focused. There is no harm in keeping in touch with people you like but who will provide you with no business benefit. After all, that's what having friends is all about. But who are the people who will help you achieve your business objectives? If you happen to like them as individuals, then this is a bonus, but there may well be people you don't really warm to but who are vital for your success. How can you best develop and maintain relationships with them? Pareto's law dictates that 80 per cent of the benefit will come from 20 per cent of the contacts. On this basis, there are probably a handful of key people you absolutely have to stay in touch with. Work out who they are and develop a strategy for maintaining your relationship with them. Be careful not to misjudge it: there's nothing worse than becoming a pain in the neck to someone. As the best form of business relationship operates on a 'give and take' basis, establish what they're getting out of it, as well as what you want. Think laterally, there may be all sorts of things that you – or other members of your network – can offer them. And remember to be human; emotional engagement and empathy are important.

As the business world moves away from the notion of using (and abusing) commodity suppliers, and towards working in strategic partnership with carefully selected organizations, you will find yourself high on the list if you have invested time in actively cultivating your network.

Chapter Twelve
Making the right impression

It's all about your profile, your position. Are you in the right meetings with the right people? Is your name at the bottom of documents and presentations? Do people know what to come to you for – and do they come to you? Or do they go to somebody else?

Nicholson McBride Office Politics Survey 2011

When we talk to people about negative politicking, many make the observation that it's the victory of style over substance. To them, it's all about coming across well, rather than actually being good at the job. And most of those people who are firmly in the Naive camp would agree: 'Why should I spend time trumpeting my successes when my results should speak for themselves? If I get my head down and do a good job, I will surely get the rewards that I deserve.' Savvy people know that this is not necessarily the case; many highly competent people get overlooked when it comes to praise, recognition and even promotion. The main reason for this is that they're ignoring an important part of their job. It's not enough just to get through the workload: you must also communicate with impact, win others over, make sure that a wide range of people are kept in the loop, and you must come across as credible. All these activities not only help to create a positive impression, they also help to ensure that good performance is recognized.

Many years ago, Albert Mehrabian came up with the 7/38/55 rule. He found that only 7 per cent of the impact of an individual's communication can be attributed to the words they use, while 38 per cent is linked to tonality – the way in which the words are spoken – and a staggering 55 per cent to body language. So, if you want to convey a message, you have to speak with impact, look the part and make sure that your delivery is congruent with the words – as well as pulling together a compelling presentation.

First impressions

Various attempts have been made to quantify precisely how long it takes for an individual to make a first impression. Some studies have demonstrated that it can take as little as seven seconds. This is especially true if you're dealing with someone who is quick to form an impression, or even judgemental. Sadly, these also seem to be the people whose good opinion, once lost, is most difficult to regain. The much quoted cliché that you never get a second chance to make a first impression describes an important truth.

Much of the advice on this front is prescriptive: do this, do that, and don't do the other! But the impression you convey must be entirely appropriate for you as a person. How do you want to come across? How would you like strangers to perceive you? Who do you want to be? You need clarity and consistency to give yourself a decent chance.

In the best-case scenario, when you are at your most resourceful, what are the features that define the essential you? Advertisers do this for products, but we spend surprisingly little time turning the attention on ourselves. Try this exercise:

- Think of three discrete and distinct attributes that you possess – or would ideally like to possess in the future.

- Write them in three interlocking circles.

- Then think about the combinations of these attributes: if you combine one with another, what does it amount to? Summarize this in the intersections.

- Finalize the exercise by completing the centre of the diagram. This should give you the essence of your personal brand (or ideal, future personal brand).

Worked example

FIGURE 12.1

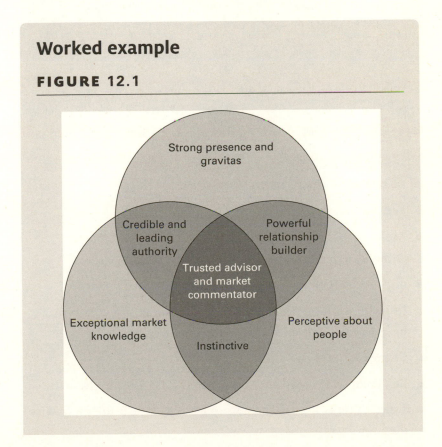

Whilst he wasn't there yet, the individual who created the diagram in Figure 12.1 realized that he needed to convey the impression of a trusted advisor and market commentator. Merely understanding this helped him; before doing this exercise, he hadn't really appreciated what he was aiming for. But beyond this, he was able to work through exactly what he would need to do in order to come across in this way. Part of it was his own belief; he needed to convince himself that he was this person, before he stood a chance of convincing others. But as well as that, he also had to display behaviours which were in keeping with his desired personal brand. And, to ensure consistency, he realized that it would take a conscious effort: all day, every day, he would need to be this person (at least at work). After a while, it started to come naturally to him. He no longer needed to think about it, since the appropriate behaviour had become automatic.

So what do you need to do to come across in the right kind of way? The answer to that question is, of course, that it depends what the right kind of way is. But here are a few tips to help you have impact:

- Be relaxed – the right mindset helps.
- Breathe – deeply and naturally.
- Make sure that your posture is appropriate – stand up straight, lengthening your spine.
- Capture the room – mentally make the space yours.
- Introduce yourself clearly – don't mumble; say what you have to say as though you're interested in it.
- Engage – make eye contact, smile and listen.
- Be perceptive – read the signs and react accordingly.
- Sound interesting – vary your pace and tone and emphasize the important words.

Shifting your reputation

Of course, whilst it's true that you don't get a second chance to make a first impression, it's a very rare individual who has never messed up at an initial meeting. But this isn't the only situation which creates a need to modify the way others perceive you. At some time or another you will, no doubt, find yourself in the position of having to shift your reputation, merely because, fairly or unfairly, you're just not perceived how you would want to be.

This is difficult enough to do when you go for it wholeheartedly – changing the way someone else thinks always is. But it's made all the more challenging if you yourself have reservations. We often hear people say that it's not even worth trying. They believe that others have long memories and rarely, if ever, change their view. Having been in the business of collecting feedback about individuals for over 20 years, I'm convinced that this is not the case – but it's a fear many people have. It may just be a convenient excuse not to try: at some level, you don't want to. Maybe it doesn't seem worth the effort, or perhaps, secretly, you like the way you're viewed. Or you may simply lack confidence; you don't think that you are going to be able to change your reputation, either because you don't possess the skills to do so or because you fear you won't live up to expectations afterwards. But whatever your concern, it is vital to overcome it before you embark on shifting others' views. It also needs to be worth it. Be clear about 'What's in it for me?' before taking any form of action.

So let's assume you've convinced yourself that you really want to shift your reputation. You must first identify what needs to change. There's a lot of talk about the value of feedback on a regular basis, and some people are fortunate enough to benefit from this. But in reality, appraisal time is when most people receive the detailed, insightful and personal feedback that is required for this type of exercise. And appraisals are few and far between. So in the meantime, how should you go about finding out what people really think about you? First, you will have your own views – a gut feel, based on what you know about yourself, and the way that others treat and respond to you. In a highly political organization, you might also have been unlucky enough to have heard bad news about yourself on the grapevine! So start the process by documenting your current impression of what others think of you. Be as honest as you can, listing both the positives and the negatives. Then add evidence to support these comments – recent successes and failures/frustrations.

Once you have done this, it's important to check it out. Ask a couple of people you trust for their insights. Stress that you want them to be honest and frank with you. If necessary, prompt them by testing out your own perceptions. Once they realize you are serious about your desire for feedback, they are more likely to start opening up to you. Make sure that you consult a range of people. Include your boss. Maybe seek some comments from customers – ideally, internal and external. Then document your summary of the feedback. What are the areas of agreement? Are there subjects on which an individual's view disagrees with your own – or with the others? Why might this be? Once you have completed this analysis, answer the following questions:

- What are my key strengths?
- How could these help me in the future?
- What are my key weaknesses or areas for development?
- How will these hinder my progress?
- Which elements of the feedback do I consider to be unfair/unsubstantiated/inaccurate?
- Why?
- What do I feel about all this?

Before moving on to the next stage, reflect on this analysis for a moment. Bear in mind the following:

- It is very important to give some thought to where the feedback comes from. Don't let yourself off the hook or make a habit of turning a blind eye to criticism, but do consider whether ulterior motives could be coming into play in some of the comments made. For instance, an entirely positive view may be driven by the fact that the person giving the feedback values your friendship and wouldn't want to hurt you. The opposite situation could also be true: an overly negative appraisal could be driven by circumstances which are more to do with the other person's feelings and motivations than your performance.

- It is always a good idea to lead from strength and plan for a future based around what you do well. There is a contrary element in all of us that wishes we could be something we're not. But we should play to our strengths. After all, you can teach a turkey to climb a tree, but it's cheaper to hire a squirrel!

- In terms of your areas for development, do you actually *want* to master these skills? Many square pegs are forced into round holes purely because people believe it's the only way to get a promotion. But you do have to demonstrate some interest and aptitude to do a job well. What really interests you?

- Challenge yourself about any seemingly unfair or historical perceptions. Are there things you still do that could give rise to this sort of criticism? If not, why are people saying it?

- Tap into your own feelings. There could be a significant driving force behind actually making the change. Do you really want to feel hurt/depressed/angry, for exactly the same reasons, three months down the line? Don't be tempted into thinking that it doesn't matter what you do, people will always be prejudiced against you. You can do something about it. You just need the will power!

So you're clear about what the current view is. You also need to establish what you want people to believe in the future. The personal branding exercise, outlined earlier in this chapter, will help you to determine what the essence of your brand will be, but you may want to break this down yet further. Outline the shifts: what do you want to move from and to in others' minds? This will give you a sense of the gap. It's then a question of how you actually make the change.

First things first: before you start to try to convince others that they're wrong about you, you need to ensure that there is substance behind your publicity. Pioneers of Neuro-Linguistic Programming (NLP) have developed the logical levels framework. This is given in Figure 12.2.

FIGURE 12.2

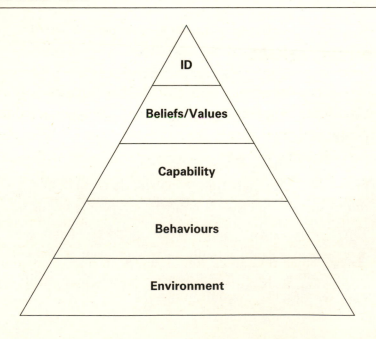

This model can help you to understand how fundamental the issues are for you and whether there is a mismatch between your view and others. Illustrations, at each level, are given below.

Identity (ID)

Although you can't alter your personality, you can change the way you view yourself – and the way in which others see you. Be honest, is the shift this fundamental for you? Does it go right to the heart of who you are? If so, the challenge is to come across as a different kind of person. So the accountant who, to date, has been utterly caught up in the technical detail of her role but wants to be seen as a client relationship manager, has to reinvent herself. The first step is for her to believe it herself. Then she needs to behave in a way which convinces others. Authenticity is critical; there is no point attempting to be seen as a new person if you don't believe it yourself, or if it sits outside your values. This leads to the next level …

Beliefs/values

Beliefs and values are also deep-seated. They drive the way you behave. What's important to you, the way you approach things and how you treat others are all driven by your beliefs and values. Changing the way others view you might well require you to shift your own thinking. Beliefs may need to change. For instance, in the example above, the accountant had always considered the technical side of her role to be more important and interesting. That was her priority. To be successful, she needs to change this belief. Reframing is an important tool if you are going to make a shift at this level. Alternatively, you may need to review what motivates you.

Capability

This relates to your core skill set, knowledge, expertise and experience – it's what you *can* do. It could be that, to address the criticism, you need to acquire new skills and enhance your capability. Picking up again on the example of the accountant, this individual might have to hone her client handling, relationship management and influencing skills – all the aspects of her work that relate to the softer, interpersonal side. Or it could be that, to get others to view her differently, she has to interact with all those people who have a negative view of her, and therefore needs to improve her networking skills.

Behaviour

This is what other people see. It's what you do. Regardless of what you have achieved at the higher levels (identity, beliefs and values, capability), since your behaviours are visible to everyone, it is vital to ensure that you act in the right kind of way. What this actually entails depends on the unique circumstances of each individual. But if you have listed your desired shifts as recommended above, it will be evident to you how you ought to modify your behaviours. This might sound simple enough, but of course it's not! It requires discipline and conscientiousness. You need to remind yourself of your new behaviours every day – or many times a day.

Environment

This applies to everything around you. It includes the culture of the organization, the ethos in the team – or what other people are saying about you. Sometimes, if you're getting bad press, it's because the way you operate, your beliefs and values, and even your character, are out of kilter with your environment. And, if you can't change it, you probably need to think about moving on. However, if it's merely a question of adjusting others' views, this is where your personal publicity campaign should start. You need to establish who the opinion formers are. Some of these will be the people who hold the negative view of you; others will be advocates; and a few won't hold any opinion of you at all – yet. Who are the people you have to impress? For every shift you've identified, you then need to think about what would convey that impression to the key people.

Consider the following:

- What evidence do you have that you can bring into play?

- Are there people out there who will vouch for you?

- What access do you have to the opinion formers? How could you gain access to them?

- What further actions can you take, which not only address the criticisms in substance but also visibly demonstrate to others that you've changed?

- Do you need to take direct action, in other words actually tell someone that you have changed?

- What feedback do you need in order to feel confident that others' perceptions are changing?

- How can you use this feedback to shift views further?

Two final thoughts. First, remember that Rome wasn't built in a day. The evidence from 360° feedback exercises suggests that, from the moment when someone starts doing something differently, it may take weeks for people to notice, months for them to entertain the possibility that the change will be lasting, and even longer for them to acknowledge this in a formal feedback collection exercise. Since it takes time to rebuild a reputation, particularly if the shift is a major one, it may make sense to map out the transition over time. Suppose you want to address a perception problem over a six-month period, where should you aim to be after one month, three months and so on? Setting these milestones not only indicates whether you are on track, it will also reduce a task which seems daunting into one which is more manageable.

The second point relates to setbacks. You might find that some of your plans fail to achieve the desired effect and you have to change tack. Or you feel as though you've let yourself down in some way – by not carrying out your actions, for example. It is vital to view these as inevitable glitches rather than reasons to stop trying.

CASE STUDY

Part of Dan's role involved presenting, once a month, to the most senior people in the organization. Whilst normally quite confident, Dan would feel very anxious before these meetings. He would overprepare. And when he presented, he would mumble, and go into far too much detail. The senior audience would switch off and, on one occasion, they actually stopped Dan before he was a third of the way through his slides. In his appraisal, Dan was told that he had a huge PR job to do. He had developed a reputation for being unimpressive, non-strategic and lacking polish. He needed to change. Bearing in mind the logical levels, Dan established that the issue was not at identity level; in other circumstances, he presented well. But his beliefs were unhelpful: he usually told himself that he was nervous, that he would make a mess of the presentation and that he needed to go into a great deal of detail to convince the audience that he knew his stuff. This, of course, became a self-fulfilling prophesy – he came across as nervous, went into far too much detail and did make a mess of the presentation. He tried reframing his thinking. Instead of feeling nervous, he convinced himself that he was excited (the physiological symptoms are very similiar). He gave himself a pep talk: he knew his stuff, he needn't go into too much detail, he just needed to relax. He imagined himself sitting around a table and conveying the same information to close colleagues. This really helped. Finally, he had to address the 'polish' issue. He observed what senior people did who could be described as having polish – how did they come across, what did they wear, and so on. He decided that it would be inappropriate to mimic them entirely, but created his own version. And he made sure that he was breathing deeply, to help relax him. It worked and he got positive feedback after the very next meeting. He then just needed to maintain this.

Checklist for change

Before embarking on your programme of change, take a look at the 10 points below. How confident are you that you can tick these off? The more positive you can be, the more likely your transition is to be successful.

1 Are you clear about what you're moving towards (vision/brand)?

2 Do you understand your reasons for changing?

3 Are you motivated to change?

4 Do you believe that change is possible?

5 Have you decided exactly what needs to change – and at what level(s) the change will occur?

6 Are you prepared for the likely consequences of change?

7 Have you thought through how you will measure success?

8 Do you know your audience?

9 Do you understand the steps you need to take?

10 Have you considered how you will sustain your own momentum and survive setbacks?

Answer yes to all of these questions, and you're ready to enhance both your savvy and your personal brand equity.

Chapter Thirteen
Summary

Savvy is the ability to engage with and handle office politics. Our research indicates that politicking has become more widespread in this millennium, largely due to recessionary times, the pace of change and the way in which technology has revolutionized the way we work – and live. So people believe that political savvy is more critical today than it has ever been, if you want to influence others, manage your career and feel fulfilled at work. This doesn't mean, though, that the increase is necessarily a bad thing. Office politics is merely the informal, rather than the formal, way of getting things done – which can be positive or negative. It depends on both the motives of the individual in question and the methods they employ. A study of this, over time, will indicate whether the individual you're dealing with is a Machiavellian or a Barbarian (who both have negative motivation) or someone who's merely a Naive (whose heart is in the right place but whose methods can be ineffective). The Star is the person who is both well motivated *and* highly successful in achieving results – for the business, for the team and for themselves.

A thorough understanding of yourself, and others, is important if you are to stand a chance of handling tricky situations well. But you also need to adopt a positive, proactive approach. There is no point burying your head in the sand, crossing your fingers and hoping that all will work out. That would be the Naive's way! You have to be alert to circumstances that might become problematic, take steps to eliminate these issues *before* they arise, and if that proves impossible, tackle them effectively. The trick is to reframe your thinking: rather than telling yourself 'There's nothing I can do,' you would be better off turning this around into something like 'What *can* I do to influence the situation and solve the problem?'

So once you are determined to have a positive impact on events, there are a whole host of skills and behaviours you need to acquire if you are to be truly savvy. The chapters in this book outline what these are, but here's a checklist. How well do you fare?

- Are you confident that, if you identify negative behaviours in the workplace – evidence of Machiavellians, Barbarians or even Naives – you have the tools and the energy to deal with them?

- Do you possess a full portfolio of influencing techniques, and the interpersonal skills to pull them off?

- When conflict arises, do you tackle it – at the right time, appropriately and usually effectively?

- Do you build and maintain robust working relationships with a wide range of different people as a normal part of your working life?

- When these relationships break down, do you know what to do – both when you're personally involved and when the rift involves others?

- Are you skilful when it comes to managing up the line: your boss, your boss's boss and maybe even beyond?

- Can you spot bullying behaviours, and more importantly address them?

- Are you confident that, given your objectives, your network is sufficiently robust – and you have the skills to maintain and expand it?

- Does your reputation in your business reflect how you want to be perceived?

If the answer to all of these questions is yes, then you can be described as being truly savvy. If not, which are the areas in which you need to improve? Are you clear about whether this will require you to acquire new skills, or is it more a question of attitude? Can you make the shift by modifying your behaviours, or will you need to change the way in which you view yourself? Being clear about the level at which the development need sits will help you to address it in the most effective – and enduring – way.

Finally, you need to develop a good sense of perspective. Many of the examples of negative politicking that we encounter can be distressing in the extreme. But standing back, viewing the situation objectively and deciding how important it really is can be invaluable. Influence where you can – even if it's just a tiny shift in a positive direction – and try not to worry about issues that you stand no chance of affecting, no matter how hard you try. In other words, be savvy about becoming more savvy.

Appendix
What kind of
politician are you?

'He's a political animal' is a statement you hear all the time. But how many times have you heard someone admit 'I am a political animal'? It's not companies that create politics, it's the people within them. So somebody must be at it! Are you? How savvy are you? Try the quiz below to assess your own political savvy, or log on to **www.officepoliticssurvey.com**.

To what extent do the statements in Table A.1 represent your philosophy? Against each statement, award yourself 2 if you completely agree, 1 if you somewhat agree and 0 if you disagree. Be honest – if you cheat, you'll only be deceiving yourself!

TABLE A.1

	Score		Score		Score		Score
1. I try to make others feel important by openly praising their work.		2. I understand where the power really lies in the organization.		3. I have used underhand methods to beat the competition.		4. I am often surprised by the way things turn out.	
5. My main priority is to help the team achieve their goals.		6. I try to adapt my style when dealing with different types of people.		7. I think it's important to ensure I always get the personal credit for successes.		8. I don't generally play the politics well.	
9. I compromise on issues that are clearly more important to others.		10. I do favours for people so that I build relationships with them.		11. I try to avoid getting involved with controversial or risky projects.		12. People sometimes take offence at what I say.	
13. I act in accordance with my values and those of the organization.		14. Total openness is not always the best approach.		15. The grapevine can be manipulated to help you achieve your goals.		16. I don't have as much influence as I would like.	

TABLE A.1 *continued*

17. I do my best to protect others from the politics that go on around here.	18. I am adept at dealing with complex interpersonal problems.	19. I have been known to bend the truth on occasions.	20. I don't worry too much about other people's feelings when dealing with difficult issues.	
21. I avoid being totally open about people's faults, as it can hurt them badly.	22. I'm good at anticipating what might happen.	23. Divide and rule is a pretty effective management technique.	24. I don't have close relationships with many of the people in power.	
25. People who are organizationally naive can get in the way of progress.	26. Resources are limited, so it's often necessary for me to fight for funding.	27. When something goes wrong, I find out who is to blame and let others know.	28. If you have a strong argument, people will usually agree with you.	
29. I help people to save face if they make a mistake.	30. Effective networking is crucial in business these days.	31. I do favours for others so that they owe me.	32. I really can't be bothered with playing the politics.	
Column 1 total	**Column 2 total**	**Column 3 total**	**Column 4 total**	

Plot your scores on the matrix in Table A.2, remembering that zero is at the centre:

- Take your total score from column 1 and, working up from the centre, place a cross at the appropriate point on the vertical axis.
- Starting at the centre and working right, add your total from column 2 to the horizontal axis.
- Working down from the centre, mark your column 3 score on the vertical axis.
- Finally, starting at the centre and working left, add your column 4 score.
- Join the four points.

TABLE A.2

Methods

Bad								Good							

							16	Column 1 Total
							14	
							12	
							10	
	1. Naive						8	**2. Star**
							6	
							4	
Column 4 Total							2	Column 2 Total

16 14 12 10 8 6 4 2   2 4 6 8 10 12 14 16

							2	
							4	
							6	
							8	Column 3 Total
	3. Barbarian							**4. Machiavellian**
							10	
							12	
							14	
							16	

Motives

A score of 12 or more in any one column is a high score.

A high score in column 2 suggests that you *are* a political animal, but it is important to view this in conjunction with columns 1 and 3, which indicate your *motives* for political behaviour.

A high score in column 1 suggests you are interested in making progress and helping the team – a Star, perhaps.

Column 3 is more to do with seeking personal gain – 12 indicates a Machiavellian/Barbarian on a grand scale, but beware if you have 8 or more in this column.

A high score in column 4 indicates that you are not at all a political animal but that you would benefit from learning some lessons in how to make happen what you want to happen. Again, this scale needs to be viewed in conjunction with columns 1 and 3, which indicate your *motives*.

A high score in column 1 suggests you are well intentioned, perhaps more Naive than Barbarian. Again, watch out for a high score in column 3.

So what does it mean? Use the following guide to get a feel for where you fall on the diagram in Figure A.1.

FIGURE A.1

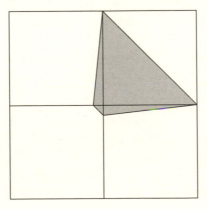

Perfect Star

There's not a lot you don't know about making things happen in the most positive way. But put it to the test and ask someone else to complete the questionnaire about you – just in case they don't share your view!

FIGURE A.2

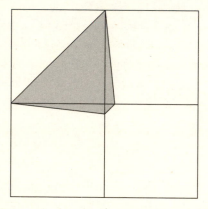

Absolute Naive

Your heart is certainly in the right place, but there's a huge amount you could do to improve your effectiveness and get better results.

FIGURE A.3

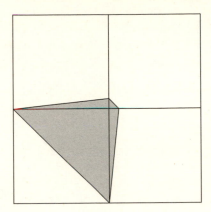

Utter Barbarian

You need to examine your motives for doing things – and how you operate. Do you want to stay in this box? You don't have to!

FIGURE A.4

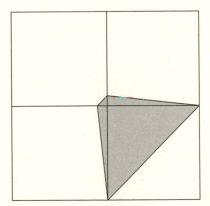

Complete Machiavellian

You firmly believe that the end justifies the means and are excellent at manipulating situations and people to get what you want. But what are you fighting for? Why not put your skills to better use and try to achieve something for the good of the whole organization?

FIGURE A.5

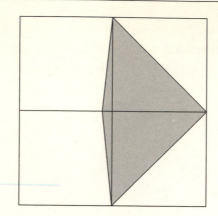

Confirmed Politician

You are effective and influential, but sometimes your motives are sound and sometimes they're not. Could it be that you're more interested in playing the game than in the result itself? Try to reduce 'below the line' activity to clean up your act.

FIGURE A.6

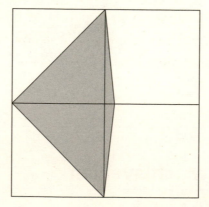

Incompetent Tinker

You like to make things happen, but somehow your actions don't seem to pay off. Try to focus your efforts 'above the line' and learn how to make things happen more smoothly and effectively.

FIGURE A.7

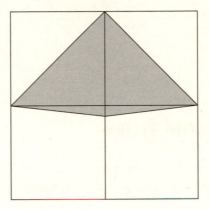

Well-meaning Activist

You are always fighting for a cause – often unselfishly – but sometimes you go about it in a clumsy or incompetent way. Keep on fighting, but give some thought to how you can achieve a win–win situation more often.

FIGURE A.8

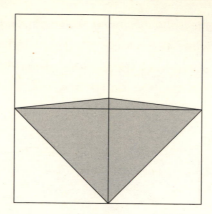

Unpredictable Snake

You are not interested in the good of the whole, nor in win–win situations. Your motives are sadly suspect. Your actions can sometimes be transparent to others, but at other times not. Examine both your methods and your motives.

FIGURE A.9

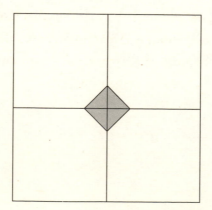

Passive Force

You don't do anyone any harm, but then you don't do much good either. You are more of a reactive than a proactive force. Think about how you could have more impact, focusing, of course, on moving up and right on the matrix towards the Star category.

FIGURE A.10

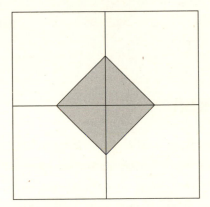

Embryonic Player

You have the potential to do more. You also have the potential to move in any direction. Analyse how you could make more of a difference in a positive way and how you could reduce any traces of incompetence or selfish motives.

FIGURE A.11

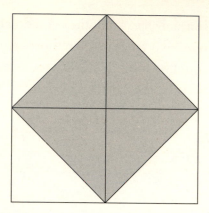

Loose Cannon

High scores on all four scales would be unusual indeed, but if you do fall into this category you need to analyse your actions carefully. In what situations do you act in a well intentioned way? What causes you to do otherwise? Similarly, when would you be an influential force and when would you bungle it?

Most of these represent the extremes, and you are unlikely to fall precisely into one category. Broadly speaking, you would be looking to eliminate any motivations that fall into the bottom half of the matrix and push your scores along the positive methods scale to enhance your effectiveness. But you shouldn't rely on this tool alone. Nor be complacent if you happen to fall into the Star camp. Being savvy involves constant observation, review and examination, of situations and people. If you want to make the most of your opportunities in the workplace, and maximize your contribution, you need to build your savvy over the course of your entire working life.

References

Covey, S (1989) 7 *Habits of Highly Effective People*, Simon & Schuster Ltd, London

Field, T, http://www.bullyonline.org/, Accessed 2012

Gittel, R J and Vidal, A (1998) *Community organizing: Building social capital as a development strategy*, Sage Publications, California

Gladwell, M (2000) *The Tipping Point: How little things can make a big difference*, Abacus, USA

McAvoy, B R and Murtagh, J (2003) 'Workplace bullying: The silent epidemic. Those who can do; those who can't, bully', *British Medical Journal*, Published 12 April 2003

Mehrabian, A (1972) *Non-verbal communication*, Aldine Transaction, London

Merrill R, Covey, S and Merrill R (1994) *First things first: Coping with the increasing demands of the workplace*, Simon & Schuster, London

Nicholson McBride Office Politics Survey 2011, http://www.officepoliticssurvey.com/about/, Accessed 2012

Prentis, D 'Bullying in the workplace on the rise' by Afua Hirsch, legal affairs editor guardian.co.uk, Monday 4 January 2010

Rayner, C and Hoel, H, cited in McAvoy, B R and Murtagh, J (2003) 'Workplace bullying: The silent epidemic. Those who can do; those who can't, bully', *British Medical Journal*, Published 12 April 2003

Seligman, Prof M (1975) *Helplessness: On depression, development, and death*. A series of books in psychology, W H Freeman/Times Books/ Henry Holt & Co, New York

Thomas, K W and Kilmann, R H (1977) 'Developing a Forced-Choice Measure of Conflict-Handling Behavior: The "Mode" Instrument', *Educational and Psychological Measurement* 37 (2), pp 309–25, Downloaded from http://epm.sagepub.com

US Department of Health and Human Services, Leadership Competencies Executive, http://hhsu.learning.hhs.gov/competencies/ leadership-political_savvy.asp, Accessed 2012

Index

NB: page numbers in *italic* indicate figures or tables